# PROFICIENT to
# Distinguished
## Mastering the T-TESS

Wesley D. Hickey
Yanira Oliveras-Ortiz

# Kendall Hunt
publishing company

Cover images taken by Rebecca Pagitt
Modeling by Jessica Pierce

# Kendall Hunt
### publishing company

www.kendallhunt.com
*Send all inquiries to:*
4050 Westmark Drive
Dubuque, IA 52004-1840

Printed in the United States of America

# CONTENTS

Most Texas teachers who started at the turn of the twenty-first century have only been evaluated by an appraisal system that had little impact on their professional growth, the Professional Development and Appraisal System (PDAS). After 2 years of piloting and refinement, the Texas Teacher Evaluation and Support System (T-TESS) was rolled out across the state in August 2016. While the piloting teachers have expressed the positive impact the new system has had on their teaching, for thousands who are new to T-TESS, the rubric is intimidating. But teachers are not alone; their principals are not only responsible for implementing this new teacher evaluation, but they will also be appraised by a new system. For the first time in Texas history, principals across the state will be evaluated using a state-developed system—the Texas Principals Evaluation and Support System (T-PESS). The T-PESS will not be covered in this book, but many of the indicators for principals relate to their effectiveness in supporting teachers. This fits well into the administrative purpose of the T-TESS.

The idea of being evaluated with a new tool and mastering the expectations of a 16-dimension T-TESS rubric is scary. The fact that principals have to master T-TESS and also the 21 indicators of the T-PESS rubric is outright overwhelming. So in an effort to support administrators and teachers, to help them move from proficient to distinguished, we have taken a close a look at each dimension and what it would look like in action. In each chapter, you'll find:

- The T-TESS rubric definition of the dimension, which is found in italics at the top of each chapter (Texas Education Agency, 2016)
- An overview of the dimension

- A look of the dimension in action
- Three big ideas to help you plan for success
- Points to remember about the dimension
- Questions for administrators to consider when observing and collecting evidence for the dimension
- Ideas related to each dimension to help you grow professionally

# Understanding T-TESS and the Distinguished Performance Level

When thinking about the rubric, it is important to remember that while there are 16 separate T-TESS dimensions, they have a high degree of interconnectedness. The dimensions do not stand alone. For example, teachers' efforts to improve differentiation of learning will impact the planning domain, particularly the activities and knowledge of student dimensions, as well as classroom culture within the instruction domain. Efforts of teachers working to improve their instructional strategies will also impact behavior linked to standards and alignment, data and assessments, activities, content knowledge and expertise, communication, differentiation and monitor and adjust. So when teachers are looking for areas to work on, they should consider which descriptors connect to other dimensions. Teachers should begin by strengthening the skills that will have the biggest impact on their instruction and their students' learning.

As teachers study the different dimensions, they will notice how frequently we mention student-centered or student ownership. Within the T-TESS rubric, lessons in which students take ownership of their learning are highly regarded. Understanding the gradual release of the responsibility model (Pearson & Gallagher, 1983) will be key to teachers as they work to implement the instructional practices valued by T-TESS and the Texas Teacher Standards. Through gradual release, lessons systematically move from teacher-directed to student-centered; from direct teach where the teacher has sole responsibility of student learning to collaborative and independent tasks where the responsibility shifts to the students. When we look at the T-TESS rubric, there is a pattern among the practices deemed distinguished. During distinguished lessons, students have ownership of their learning and behavior. In proficient lessons there is a shared responsibility between teachers and students. In distinguished lessons, the responsibility shifts toward the students while the teachers serve as facilitators of learning rather than being solely responsible for student learning.

It is important to remember that giving students ownership of their learning will begin to shift the lessons and the classroom culture but it will not automatically guarantee a distinguished rating. The evidence linked to each of the dimensions will determine the rating. But, there is an important data point that will influence the performance level of the lessons—the impact teachers' actions have on students' mastery of the learning objective. Teachers must monitor the impact of the planned lesson, the instruction, and activities on student learning. If there is no evidence that student-centered lessons have positively impacted the students' understanding and mastery of the learning objectives, then the rating of the lessons will be negatively impacted. There must be evidence that the activities have successfully helped the students understand and master the objectives. Execution of the lesson is key as is the students' mastery of the learning goals.

## The Big T-TESS Characteristics

The T-TESS is designed as an instrument for improving teacher performance. As with any professional activity, a few behaviors make the biggest difference. This is often known as the 80/20 principal, suggesting that 80% of an outcome is often the result of 20% of behaviors. This is not to say that 80% of what a teacher does is unimportant; in fact, refining the art and science of teaching makes a huge difference in student achievement. The T-TESS requires this of distinguished teachers.

That being said, this book attempts to simplify the rubric, and the following outlines the nine most important components of the T-TESS. This is the big picture:

- Plan with purpose and detail.
- Get students actively involved with effective and efficient procedures.
- Develop character in students.
- Guide students toward taking personal ownership in their education.
- Bridge instruction to multiple contexts; and if you are in a tested subject, this includes the STAAR/EOC.
- Monitor, and have students monitor their own, progress.
- Use data to find gaps and weaknesses in instruction and address them.
- Connect with parents and community members.
- Always get better … be your own best coach.

This evaluation instrument is designed to create an atmosphere of professional growth and support. This can only happen with teacher and principal acceptance, understanding that having a path for improvement is more important than a high score.

Pearson, P. D., & Gallagher, M. (1983). The instruction of reading comprehension. *Contemporary Educational Psychology, 8,* 317–344.

Texas Education Agency. (2016). *T-TESS Teacher Handbook.* Retrieved from https://teachfortexas.org/Resource_Files/Guides/T-TESS_Teacher_Handbook.pdf

# Planning

**Dimension 1.1:** Standards and Alignment

**Dimension 1.2:** Data and Assessment

**Dimension 1.3:** Knowledge of Students

**Dimension 1.4:** Activities

# Standards and Alignment

*The teacher designs clear, well-organized, sequential lessons that reflect best practice, align with standards, and are appropriate for diverse learners.*

A 2011 story in the journal *District Administration* describes the strategy of Celina, Texas, in improving alignment of the curriculum (Herbert, 2011). Curriculum director Lizzy Kloiber's initiative was to use coaches to get everyone on the same page in regard to the standards that students were expected to know. This included developing an understanding of the knowledge and skills students learned before going into a grade and prerequisites that must be learned in the current classrooms to prepare for success at the next level.

Dr. Kloiber used master teachers to improve preparation on the standards, and this was done for one simple reason: The first step to any lesson is preparing the students for what they will be held accountable for knowing. The increased curriculum clarity in Celina continues to provide a strong foundation for academic success.

The Texas Essential Knowledge and Skills (TEKS) should drive the lesson planning and the instruction of every teacher in Texas public schools (Texas Education Agency, 2016). By analyzing the content, context, cognitive expectations, and required depth of knowledge of the standards, teachers can develop lessons that are closely aligned to the TEKS and ultimately to the state's assessments. Additionally, when teachers have a strong understanding of the standards, they can write strong, standard-based learning objectives while developing lessons and designing learning activities that are well organized and sequential. And since the STAAR and EOC are based on these standards, the process prepares students for the tests.

Teachers that have a good grasp of the standards they teach understand the prerequisite knowledge and skills students must have to successfully master the TEKS. Understanding the background knowledge and skills students must possess facilitates the design of lessons that are not only aligned to the TEKS, but also to the students' readiness and academic needs.

Every teacher in Texas is responsible for teaching a large number of standards. By becoming experts on the standards they teach, teachers can design units of study and activities that integrate them, and furthermore, provide cross-disciplinary understanding within multiple contexts. At the elementary level, self-contained teachers that are well versed on their standards could integrate reading standards during science and social studies lessons. They can reinforce math during a science lesson, but to design broader units of study, teachers must have a deep understanding of their standards to ensure integrated learning opportunities. Similarly, teams can support each other by designing lessons that are vertically aligned to the TEKS. Vertical alignment of the lessons ensures that students have a strong foundation in the required knowledge and skills for future grade levels and courses. This goes beyond knowing what students are expected to master at the current grade level; understanding how the standards relate to the previous and next courses ensures that the teachers within an academic department have a shared understanding of the curricular needs and instructional strategies used among the classes and disciplines.

In the twenty-first-century classrooms, technology is often an integral part. In order for teachers to seamlessly integrate technology, they must understand the standards and how technology could enhance learning. Technology should be integrated to enrich the teaching and learning of the standards, and not just as an add-on to the lessons. Teachers moving from proficient to distinguished will make the connection with TEKS to technology appear seamless.

# A Brief Look at 1.1 in Action

The third grade team meets to plan math for the upcoming week. The teachers have the results of the unit's pre-assessment and have shared concerns regarding certain prerequisite standards that need to be addressed. Ms. Rojas, the team leader, leads the team discussion and discusses how the multiplication unit will be structured. The teachers begin planning for the unit by deconstructing all the standards that will be taught, including 3.4.E—multiplication. After deconstructing the standards, they determine how mastery of the standards will be assessed.

Once the team agrees upon the end of the unit assessment, each teacher groups the students based on the pre-assessment results. The team designs different activities to scaffold learning and address the needs of the various groups of students. The students who have not mastered, according to the pre-assessment, the basic concept of multiplication would work on hands-on activities to build on their understanding of repeated addition and the concept of multiplication. Students who have the prerequisite skills and are ready to work at the level of the TEKS will work on activities at the level of the standards, while the students who have shown mastery of the standards will work on enrichment activities, integrating the process standards vertically aligned to fourth grade TEKS. By designing activities at various levels, teachers are using their understanding of students' strengths and needs to provide appropriate activities to facilitate deeper learning of the content and student success. The lesson designed by Ms. Rojas is not only aligned to the standards but also to the academic needs of diverse students.

While Domain 1 is focused on planning, all the dimensions within the domain go beyond the planning phase of a lesson. Distinguished teachers show their instructional expertise by masterfully executing the plans.

# The Big Three

This dimension is the foundation of them all. Teachers can do everything else at the highest level, but if they do not have instruction aligned with the TEKS, it does not help in preparing the students for how they will be held accountable. Great instruction with the wrong standards results in poor performance. Fundamentally, there are three actions that teachers must take for Dimension 1.1.

1. In planning, start with the Texas Essential Knowledge and Skills. Activities, assignments, classroom work, and assessments must be driven by the TEKS.

2. Curriculum guides may be used, too, but there needs to be some professional friction between the instructor and this resource. Teachers who blindly follow the curriculum guide of the district are not using professional discretion, which once again, must start with the TEKS. Furthermore, students are unique and have needs that must be addressed in the planning and teaching of the lessons.

3. Understanding the TEKS to design lessons closely aligned to the standards is key to the success of any lesson. Equally important is ensuring that assessments measure the content, context, and cognitive expectations to the TEKS. Teachers must develop assessments in which students have to apply the acquired knowledge and skills in different contexts and at the appropriate depth of knowledge. Alignment of instruction with the TEKS is a start, but it must continue to assessment. Aligning TEKS to the assessment is more that checking for content knowledge, but the instructor must determine if the student knows the TEKS in a variety of contexts in order to meet state requirements.

## Points to Remember

- The lesson planning process must begin with the standards.
- Teachers must take the time to analyze the standards to understand the expectations of each as well as the alignment to other disciplines in the same grade level, previous and future courses.
- Lesson alignment to the standards ensures preparation for the state assessments.
- The lesson must be designed and executed to facilitate learning of standards in a logical sequence.
- When teachers have a deep understanding of the standards, their students' academic background, and needs, they are able to design and teach standard-based lessons that are relevant and address the students' needs.
- The design of standards-based lessons that take students' academic needs into account build a strong foundation for differentiated learning.
- By designing standard-based lessons that address the students' academic needs, teachers can facilitate student-centered learning that provides for opportunities of remediation and enrichment.
- The design and execution of lessons must provide for enough time for each lesson component—including statement of the learning objectives, the lesson, student work and reflection, and closure.
- Technology should be used as a tool to enrich students' learning opportunities.

# The Administrative Lens

During the pre-observation conference and the observation, the appraiser should consider:

- Has the teacher planned a lesson in which all the learning goals are measurable and aligned to the TEKS?
- Did the teacher plan and execute a lesson that was adequately sequenced?
- Are the planned activities, materials, and assessments relevant to students' prior knowledge?
- How did the teacher plan to integrate other content areas?
- Is the teacher aware of how the lesson's content aligns to the vertical standards and to standards in other content areas in the same grade level?
- Is the teacher aware of the students' academic needs?
- How does the lesson address the students' academic needs? Does the teacher provide opportunities for remediation and enrichment?
- In what ways is the teacher planning to use technology to enhance learning of the standards?

# Moving from Proficient to Distinguished

There are several resources related to Dimension 1.1 that most districts already possess. TEKS resources and other curriculum guides are a good starting point. But there needs to be some intellectual friction between any curriculum guide and teachers; blind adherence is not a good thing. Critiquing the plan, and improving upon it, must happen for increased understanding of the standards and alignment. Teachers are well-educated professionals that are too important to give any verbatim plan.

Beyond a strong understanding of the TEKS in one's subject or grade, distinguished teachers will be aware of the knowledge and skills that their students should know in both the grade below and above. This allows instructors to recognize any potential gaps as the student enters the grade, and ensures a strong academic foundation for future classes. Awareness of other grade level TEKS also helps teachers design lessons that are aligned to the students' needs while addressing missing prerequisite knowledge and skills or while enriching the advanced students' learning experiences.

Beyond the TEKS, teachers need to know their students. Reading books and going to training sessions related to connecting with students from different backgrounds can provide more nuanced approaches to impacting students with the curriculum. Distinguished teachers are committed to knowing their students to better meet their academic needs.

Distinguished teachers understand the importance of backwards planning and after studying the standards, begin the planning process by designing assessments that are rigorous and closely aligned to the TEKS. In order to facilitate vertical alignment, teachers should work with their teams in the design of assessments. Thereafter, they should collaborate in the design of lessons that are appropriately sequenced and are relevant to their students, keeping in mind individual student needs and interests to increase student engagement.

The planning of the lessons is only the beginning of the teaching cycle; while executing the plans, teachers must be aware of their students' progress to facilitate the appropriate implementation of the lesson cycle and the gradual release model. By being aware of the students' needs and progress, distinguished teachers can ensure the successful implementation of the lesson plan. They pace the lesson cycle and the gradual release model to ensure students have adequate time to work at each stage of the lesson. Teachers who spend time observing colleagues can learn how to improve their teaching practices and the implementation of strong lessons.

Impacting students has to include understanding the standards in multiple contexts. For teachers within a state tested subject, curriculum alignment that is embedded in assessment is important. Professional development on question writing, and how to use these questions to challenge, motivate, and educate, is an important step in the preparation process.

Herbert, M. (2011, October 1). A small community's innovative curriculum coaches. *District Administration*, 36–38.

Texas Education Agency. (2016). *Texas essential knowledge and skills*. Retrieved from http://tea.texas.gov/index2.aspx?id=6148

# Data and Assessment

*The teacher uses formal and informal methods to measure student progress, then manages and analyzes student data to inform instruction.*

The concept of data-driven decision making has been in vogue for the past decade, created in part by advances in technology that allow for increased analysis of information. Educators throughout Texas check data charts in systems such as DMAC and Eduphoria that provide information on individual student and class performance according to a multitude of variables. In fact, many schools go too far, sending information to teachers and administrators that are poorly understood, suggesting the need for simplification or training.

The use of data to make decisions is the cornerstone of response to intervention (RTI). RTI looks at the progress of students, and if there are gaps, provides targeted remediation. This is the formal routine of the school, but effective teachers continually measure the competency of students as a standard is taught. In fact, no one in the school should know as much about the academic progress of students as their teachers.

Formative assessments provide ongoing knowledge of the success of students at understanding the standards. Teachers who walk around, watch work being done, question students, and generally watch for signs of struggle are likely to have a good idea if there is an appropriate grasp of the concept or skill. Additionally, teachers must use written formative and summative assessments, preferably developed by the team to ensure the alignment of the expectations across all classrooms, to assess students' progress. Formative assessments should be used to adjust instruction for the remaining lessons of the unit while summative assessments should be used to determine the need to revisit certain concepts as the teachers continue to teach the district's curriculum.

The use of data to drive instruction is the foundation of this second dimension of the planning domain. Teachers must help students understand their own progress; teachers must empower students to self-monitor so each child understands his or her own strengths and needs. Systems should be in place to facilitate students tracking their own progress; students should be informed of their progress and receive feedback from their teachers on a regular basis. While it is important that the teachers are aware of their students' progress and needs, it is imperative that students also have a strong understanding of their own progress. Distinguished teachers put systems in place to ensure students take ownership of their learning.

While data assessment is generally used to identify students' needs and strengths, teachers must use the formative and summative assessment data to reflect on their own practices. Distinguished teachers understand the impact their own instructional strengths and weaknesses have on their students' success. They understand their instructional weakness, as reflected by the data, and seek ideas from those whose data show those areas are strengths. Distinguished teachers use data to identify areas in which they have to grow professionally.

It is important to note that while teachers must assess their students using authentic assessments that measure students' progress within each unit of study, teachers who teach core subjects, assessed by STAAR/EOC, must help students see the relationship to the test by bridging the instructional activities to multiple-choice STAAR/EOC formatted questions. A plan for interleaving STAAR/EOC questions into the lesson is a good strategy for collecting formative data on student understanding. It forces the students, either in groups or individually, to continually view the competency in the way in which the individual (and campus) will ultimately be held accountable. STAAR/EOC test time is like game day, and no coach would ever send a team on the field of play without having spent enough time mimicking the actual game to provide a comfortable understanding of skills and strategies that will be used. Drills are fine, but students need to put the skills into a game like situation. The game that teachers prepare for in most classrooms is the STAAR/EOC.

Game day assessment is continued by including these types of questions on at least part of classroom tests. Teachers evaluate competency in a number of ways, which is important, but the state has set for us an academic goal, along with the rules of play. There should be no surprises on the day of the STAAR/EOC. Classroom teachers will already know and have developed the skill level of each student.

# A Brief Look at 1.2 in Action

Mrs. Roberts consistently collects data on her students, both formal and informal. The campus benchmarks have their purpose, but she has a good idea how the students will perform long before she sees the results. Her plans for the lesson include purposeful group designations based upon student needs as evidenced by the data, as well as a plan to collect information specific for the standard being taught. Although Dimension 1 is related to the planning she does prior to class, the execution below shows how things were carried out, which will impact the rating of this dimension.

Mrs. Roberts was having the students work on graphs in small groups within her second-grade classroom. The TEKS objective being developed was 2.10(b), "Organize a collection of data with up to four categories using pictographs and bar graphs with intervals of one or more." The students were recording their data of the number of insects found in multiple square-meter plots on the playground. This connected with a lesson in science inquiry that was completed the day before.

Mrs. Roberts walked around the room and corrected several students on the appropriate way to set up the x and y axes, but overall, the students were doing well. She went deeper and asked several students to explain how to make a bar graph that illustrated the favorite foods of students in the class. What about favorite foods of everyone in the school, she queried.

Before she transitioned into an assignment where a bar graph was made with manipulatives, she handed out a STAAR formatted question on a notecard and had them answer as a group. This only took 2 minutes, but it provided her some valuable formative data as she heard the discussions in breaking down the question. She knew a class test at the end of the week would provide for further analysis of needs.

# The Big Three

Using data to inform instruction is an important part of a professional teacher's repertoire, and there is a lot of data out there. In fact, there may be too much, which creates noise that has little meaning. If you do nothing else, remember to do the following:

1. Have an easily understood and highly meaningful data chart. The chart should be simple enough that an elementary student could quickly determine its meaning. Students should track their own progress toward mastery of the learning objectives while teachers use the data to monitor their own instructional strengths and weakness.

2. Any lesson that does not have over 70% of students indicating mastery of the concept should be retaught using a different strategy. The variance in instruction should keep the students who understand interested and provide another context for those who are struggling. Targeted interventions can be used on students when less than 30% are not grasping the standard.

3. Core subject teachers who are also responsible for preparing students for STAAR/EOC should consistently bridge instruction with the STAAR/EOC. There are numerous stories of teachers who gave up on highly engaging instructional practices because the students began to have difficulty with the STAAR. The reason is that the STAAR does not require a hands-on understanding of the skill but rather an abstract understanding at the appropriate depth of knowledge, which means that students need to see the standard in an objective format similar to the state tests.

# Points to Remember

- Monitoring through proximity to students is important. Teachers can recognize problems and intervene quickly while purposefully walking around the classroom.
- Collecting data on STAAR/EOC questions does not have to be through formal benchmarks. Interleaving these questions into general instruction and including them on traditional classroom tests can provide a wealth of information regarding student understanding.
- Data collected not only provides information on the student, but it also helps teachers understand the effectiveness of the lesson.
- Students should graph the results of their efforts for each standard. Each student should eventually take control of his or her own learning, so data-driven

decision making should be required of students, as well. A student should not go to tutoring without knowing why.

- Keeping parents aware of progress is important. Students should be required to show their parents their progress. Most districts have parent portals to make this easy, so it is important to keep it accurate and up to date.
- Teachers should keep records of classroom data analysis to share with the principal. The dimension is determined through several sources of evidence, but a good data notebook would be beneficial in indicating strength in this area.

## The Administrative Lens

An administrator conducting a pre-observation conference and providing evaluation to a teacher should consider:

- Does the teacher have a plan to monitor student work during the lesson?
- Does the teacher have a plan to recognize student errors and provide effective feedback during the lesson?
- How do students monitor their own progress toward mastery of the objectives?
- Is there evidence that assignments are graded promptly with effective feedback to the student?
- Does the teacher use the data to plan targeted instruction both individually and overall?
- Is there evidence that the teacher uses data to evaluate the effectiveness of lessons?
- Does the communication between teachers and students support increased understanding of the material?

## Moving from Proficient to Distinguished

Quantitative analysis is an area of which many teachers feel unprepared. This is why many teachers compliantly accept the reports given from the curriculum directors but privately admit they do not totally understand them. As we said earlier, having the simplest and most meaningful reports possible can be an excellent tool (especially for administrators), but there are some slick ways to look at some of the data. The Internet is full of lessons.

The analysis of data should not be done in isolation; there are powerful lessons to learn when a team comes together to analyze assessment data and use it to adjust instruction for future lessons. Even if a structure is not in place at the campus, teachers can take the initiative to work with others on the analysis of their data. Teachers whose actions have a big impact on student learning understand the importance of learning from others. When professional learning communities (PLCs) are implemented as originally intended, the structure imbedded within those meetings provides teachers with powerful information about the impact their teaching is having on student learning and what to do for students who struggled to master the learning objectives.

Distinguished lessons are student-centered. Teachers who want to design and implement lessons at the distinguished level must find ways to encourage students to take more of a role in their learning. Try new and creative ways to get students to recognize the standards and their mastery as it relates to them. Too often students are kept in the dark regarding their progress. This should change; students should be aware and be able to speak about their own progress.

Finally, distinguished teachers know their students better than anyone else. Do not make this knowledge a secret from the principal. All teachers should be able to have a 2-minute "elevator talk" with their principal, in which standards being taught, percentage of kids who get it and the names of kids who have not achieved mastery, and intervention efforts with these kids are quickly discussed. Your principal will love you for it.

# Knowledge
# of Students

*Through knowledge of students and proven practices, the teacher ensures high levels of learning, social-emotional development, and achievement for all students.*

A *New York Times* video about Jeffrey Wright (Parker-Pope, 2012) told the story of a teacher who had a major influence on the lives his students. There was definitely an academic impact; he had a reputation as an engaging teacher who was creative and hands-on in his teaching of standards. But his influence went further. He knew about the nonacademic challenges of most of his students. The professional relationship he developed was a catalyst for developing successful students academically and socioemotionally.

He accomplished this in part through confessing to his students the disappointments, challenges, and elation of having a son with special needs. His story was sensitive, emotional, and touched his students in ways that made them reflect on their own issues. Sharing this personal testimony created a professional relationship where students were highly motivated to do well.

The lessons learned from Jeffrey Wright's story clearly show that asserting that teachers can "stand in front of the classroom and lecture about the material; if the kids do not get it, its their fault" is unacceptable. Knowledge of students means impacting them in targeted, and often subtle and individual, ways. Just about everything teachers do is purposeful, so group assignments, differentiation of the curriculum, decisions regarding who to praise publicly, and so forth, are based upon the teachers' knowledge of students.

Teachers' knowledge about standards is the foundation of every lesson; however, the successful execution of those lessons relies on the teachers' knowledge about their students' prior knowledge, academic and social-emotional needs, and their progress toward mastery of the standards. Distinguished teachers use the deep understanding of their students to modify lessons as they are executing it; ensuring that the students' academic and social-emotional needs are addressed by preparing lessons that target those needs and adjusting the lesson as it progresses.

Furthermore, teachers who have a deep understanding of their students are able to plan lessons in which students have the opportunity to guide their own learning while using their own strengths and background knowledge to enhance learning for both self and others. The understanding of the students' strengths and needs, equally as important as understanding the TEKS, is key to the successful design and execution of standards-based lessons. In student-centered classrooms, standards and each student's strengths and needs, both academic and socio-emotional, drive the planning and instruction.

## A Brief Look at 1.3 in Action

Jimmy Caldwell had a poster on the locker room wall that said, "Failure to prepare is preparing to fail." Coach Caldwell has this philosophy both on the playing field and in the classroom. His lesson plans were always thoughtful and purposeful, in part because he believed that small improvements on a consistent basis led to large benefits over time. He often pointed to this as a major factor in both his three state football championships and six straight years without a failure on the End of Course exam.

His planning took into account student needs, both academic and socio-emotional. Lesson plans clearly outlined groups who would be working together, but would also have notes such as, "Larry responds well to Amy in small groups; learns better" or "Jennifer is struggling with the death of her aunt; don't push too hard right now." His plans were important enough that he always took a reminding glance before every class period.

His lesson plans also took into account the academic needs of students; he out-lined remedial needs for students who did not perform well on the EOC questions he regularly presented in class. There were often groups designed to handle the differentiated needs of the students; some accelerated, some worked on previous knowledge and skills. If coaching football taught him anything, it was that every kid is different. He thought that there is nothing more unfair than treating every student the same way. His lesson plans were an illustration of this belief.

## The Big Three

Having a deep knowledge of students is key to the success of any teacher. Lesson plans are only as strong as the execution of the activities and the impact the in-struction has on student learning. So when working on lesson plans, keep in mind three key points.

1. Learning does not happen in a vacuum. Take into consideration the students' academic and social-emotional needs, background knowledge, and interests when planning lessons. Teachers that show students they care will have a greater engagement and success rate than teachers who teach one way regard-less of who is seated in their classrooms.
2. Students bring a lot of experiences into the classroom; help them understand how their knowledge, skills, and personal strengths relate to learning, and give them opportunities to use those attributes to help others. Empower stu-dents to take ownership of their learning.
3. Design differentiated lessons that leverage students' learning styles. Planning with students' needs in mind will close learning gaps and increase student engagement.

## Points to Remember

- In student-centered classrooms, standards and each student's needs drive the instruction.
- Lessons need to connect with prior knowledge.
- Lessons need to connect with student interest.
- Connect instruction to the students' background and life experience when possible.
- Provide opportunities for students to learn the material in the way in which they prefer.

- Organize the classroom based upon the teachers' knowledge of student needs.
- Help students understand their own strengths and needs in order to use those to enhance their own learning as well as their classmates' learning.

## The Administrative Lens

During the pre-observation conference and the observation, the appraiser should consider:

- How well does the lesson demonstrate the teacher's knowledge about students' needs, interests, and strengths?
- How is the teacher facilitating the connection of the content to the students' prior knowledge?
- Are students given the opportunity to rely and maximize their strengths and apply their prior knowledge and experiences?
- Does the lesson allow students to learn through different learning styles aligned to their interests and learning profiles?
- How will the teacher address the students' academic and social-emotional needs throughout the lesson?
- Are students given the opportunity to lead their own learning while using their strengths and experiences to enhance learning?

## Moving from Proficient to Distinguished

Teachers can gain a basic understanding of their students' needs, interests, and background through beginning of the year surveys, ice-breaker activities, and diagnostic assessments. However, for teachers to have a significant understanding of their students, interactions must go beyond the fun beginning of the year activities and the required diagnostic assessments. Teachers must spend time engaging students in conversations to get a true picture of the life, struggles, experiences, and strengths the students bring to the classroom. They must be master of the curriculum they teach in order to assess the knowledge and skills the students need to be successful in that grade level or content area. Teachers that plan and teach proficient lessons use the gathered information about their students to connect to students' background knowledge and experiences. During a distinguished lesson, the connections go beyond background knowledge. Distinguished lessons help students understand how the content relates to their life, as well as to future learning and other content areas.

By allowing teachers to work collaboratively with other teachers in other content areas, school leaders could facilitate conversations not only about the curriculum but about students' needs, strengths, learning styles, and background. Additionally, every returning student on campus had a number of teachers the prior year who could provide important insights. While developing a deep understanding about their students is each teacher's responsibility, relying on other teachers who know the students is a way to expedite the process while building shared responsibility for student success.

During proficient lessons, the teachers adjust the lesson to address students' gaps in learning. During a distinguished lesson, students take ownership of their learning and learn to leverage their strengths and prior knowledge to enhance learning. Teachers planning distinguished lessons include opportunities for students to use strategies that address their needs, strengths, and interests. A distinguished lesson is one in which the teacher has planned activities in which students lead their own learning, and the teachers' efforts result in students who understand their own strengths and needs.

Parker-Pope, T. (2012, December 24). *Laws of physics can't trump the bonds of love.* Retrieved from http://well.blogs.nytimes.com/2012/12/24/laws-of-physics-cant-trump-the-bonds-of-love/

# Activities

*The teacher plans engaging, flexible lessons that encourage higher-order thinking, persistence, and achievement.*

Phillip Schlechty, founder of the Schlechty Center for Leadership in School Reform, states that "the art and science of teaching is found in the design of work for students that appeals to the motives they bring to that work and results in their learning what their teachers expect them to learn" (Schlechty, 2011, p. 21). This philosophy is at the heart of Dimension 1.4. This fourth dimension of the planning domain focuses on the ability of the instructor to use the standards, data regarding student needs, and knowledge of the discipline to creatively engage students with meaningful work.

Teachers developing engaging activities must start with the TEKS. A purposeful approach to the work is important, because activities can often stray from original meanings. This is not all bad, and effective teachers will allow students to lead their own learning and use this exploration to segue into other TEKS, but there must be a continued understanding of the knowledge or skill that was originally the focal point.

Once the activity aligns with the TEKS, effective teachers structure the lesson to take advantage of time, predict questions, provide for reflection and further inquiry, and require the concept be used in multiple contexts. Distinguished teachers are able to do this while creating a sense of ownership on the part of the students. Proficient teachers ask questions that engage students in critical thinking; distinguished teachers provide students with opportunity to generate their own questions, solve problems, and think critically about real-world situations. Proficient teachers plan activities to ensure that students understand their roles in the learning process; distinguished teachers plan activities in which students are responsible for holding each other accountable for learning.

Note that Domain 1 is about planning, but since educational processes tend to be interrelated, it is hard for activity planning to be separated from execution. An effective activity does not remain in the planning stage; it must be embedded within the classroom management and motivation that makes everything come together. The teachers' actions and planning must result in an effective student-centered lesson for the planning dimension to be rated as distinguished.

## A Brief Look at 1.4 in Action

Melissa Rodriguez was planning her lesson in social studies on the Alamo. She looked at TEKS 7.3c and began to develop a plan based upon that standard. She wanted to interleave several interactive activities so that the knowledge and skills being learned would be used in multiple ways, which would increase the likelihood of the student truly understanding this integral part of Texas history.

Melissa planned to briefly discuss the background of the Alamo, and she planned for a transition into an activity where the students worked together to recognize similar patterns between this historical event and the song "Remember the Alamo." She played the song in class, briefly led a classroom discussion regarding its meaning, and let the groups get together to plan a brief presentation that supported the steps of a speech the students were learning in their English class.

During the planning of the lesson, Melissa identified the students who would serve as team leaders for this activity. She regularly assigned different group leaders depending on particular student strengths and needs. She developed a launching document where she stated her expectations, which included the assignment of different activities for each member of the group to promote group and individual accountability. As part of the learning process, the team leaders would have to gather information researched by each member and combine it into a 3-minute speech on the similarities and differences between the Alamo and "Remember the Alamo." By asking the groups to research different components of the history of the Alamo to compare to the song, the teacher provided opportunities for the students to set goals and evaluate each other's work while increasing accountability. Students would be given the opportunity to take ownership of their learning while Ms. Rodriguez facilitated learning that was focused on the standards.

As part of the final project, writing of a ballad, folk, country, rock, or rap song that outlined the story and meaning of the Alamo, the groups had to generate questions about Texas history and the Alamo, and explain how those questions related to issues faced by Texans nowadays. By requiring students to include questions related to current situations in Texas, the teacher provided opportunities for critical thinking and questioning within the "real world."

The project would extend into the next day. In order to continue to give students ownership of the learning and hold each other accountable, students used Google Drive to outline and refine the song overnight. Students not only had access to the technology as a research tool, but they also had access to technology tools that facilitated the collaboration and ownership of learning.

It is important to note that when technology is not accessible, the planning of the lesson can still be rated as distinguished if there is preponderance of evidence that all other descriptors are within the distinguished level. Furthermore, the integration of technology for the sake of using technology does not move a lesson into the distinguished level; the use of technology must add value to the learning experiences and be aligned to the purpose and goals of the lesson.

# The Big Three

All teachers have struggling students in their classrooms who some might think cannot handle critical thinking, much less generate their own questions. But if we take time to listen to children outside the classrooms, we hear a constant stream of questions (Why or what does that mean? How come that happened?). Children are naturally inquisitive and teachers should leverage rather than squander that curiosity. When designing activities keep these three points in mind:

1. Teachers should come prepared to ask some higher-order thinking questions during their lessons, but most importantly, teachers should create a learning

environment where students are asking most of the questions. By allowing students to generate their own questions, teachers give students ownership of their learning.

2. Design activities that are aligned not only to the standards but also to the students' needs—scaffold instruction so students' needs are met while moving toward mastery of the standards. Keep students informed of their progress to ensure they take ownership of their learning and their progress.

3. Give students an active role in their learning by designing activities in which each child has a role in the learning process. Collaborative learning provides ample opportunities for students to set goals, reflect on their progress, and hold each other accountable for their learning.

## Points to Remember

- All activities need to be aligned to the TEKS.
- Students should be given the opportunity to generate their own questions, not just opportunities to answer higher-order thinking questions posed by the teacher.
- The use of technology in developing the activities can be an important step in moving the lesson to a distinguished level when it is used to strengthen the lesson and facilitate the students' ownership of learning.
- Develop activities so there is peer interaction, support, and accountability.
- Creating groups for working with the activities needs to be purposeful based upon the individual needs of the students.
- The activities should lead to further inquiry and depth of thinking.
- Activities should be "real world" to the extent possible.
- When planning real-world activities, students should understand the relevance of the lesson to the real world.

## The Administrative Lens

An administrator providing evaluation to a teacher should consider:

- Are the groups purposeful and based upon student needs?
- Are activities aligned with the TEKS?
- Do the activities provide for the use of knowledge and skills within different contexts?
- Is the activity relevant to the "real world"?
- Does the use of technology make sense within the activity?

- Does the activity lead to depth of understanding?
- How do the activities promote students' critical thinking?
- How are students encouraged to ask higher-order thinking questions?
- How are students encouraged to take ownership of their learning while holding each other accountable?

# Moving from Proficient to Distinguished

When planning activities for distinguished lessons, teachers have a vast number of resources available to them. First, teachers must use the district's curriculum and scope and sequence to ensure they are designing lessons that are aligned to the standards. Teachers must have a deep understanding of the standards in order to design activities with clear expectations to ensure students' efforts are aligned with the lesson's objectives.

In order to design strong lessons, teachers must leverage the human capital available at their schools. Other teachers with knowledge about the content and students they work with, and most importantly the students, are great resources in developing activities. Teachers that know their curriculum can excel at planning strong lessons that engage students in critical thinking, but it takes teachers with a deep understanding of their students' needs, strengths, background, and experiences to design lessons in which the students' background is used to maximize learning.

Teachers who collaborate benefit from other professional expertise while sharing their own skills with colleagues. The same is true of students; students who understand their own strengths and needs can leverage that understanding to enhance their learning as well as their classmates' learning. Proficient teachers are aware of their students' needs; distinguished teachers use that knowledge to design lessons that are closely aligned to the TEKS while pushing students to take responsibility for their own learning. During distinguished lessons, teachers empower their students to ask questions and hold each other accountable for learning. When teachers are first working on transitioning from teacher-led to students-led lessons, it is important for teachers to understand that students must be taught how to ask questions at higher levels of thinking related to content, how to lead their learning, how to collaborate, and how to hold themselves and their classmates accountable. When students have spent years in teacher-led classrooms, they lack the skills to self-direct, but they are capable of doing so with the appropriate instruction and classroom structures. This goes beyond the planning of student-centered lessons; students must be taught how to engage in student-led instruction.

Proficient teachers are aware of the importance of making learning relevant to life outside the classrooms. Teachers who plan and execute distinguished lessons understand how to integrate real-world application related to the content in their classrooms. The planning of lessons where students apply their knowledge and skills to real-world problems requires a deep understanding of the curriculum and of students' prior knowledge and experiences. In a distinguished lesson, students clearly understand when and how the knowledge and skills learned through the activities will be needed in the real world. Distinguished teachers plan lessons where learning does not take place in a vacuum but rather in the context of the world and community in which the student lives. Developing lessons that provide opportunities to apply learning to the real world are challenging to develop; teachers should work together to leverage the expertise and ideas of others within their department or team.

The fourth dimension in the planning domain also addresses the use of technology as an instructional tool. While technology can make learning rigorous and relevant, distinguished teachers understand that technology must be used to enhance learning and not as an add-on to simply use the technology. A distinguished lesson can be planned and executed without technology if all other descriptors within the dimension are present.

Schlechty, P. C. (2011). *Engaging students: The next level of working on the work.* San Francisco, CA: Jossey-Bass.

# Instruction

**Dimension 2.1:** Achieving Expectations

**Dimension 2.2:** Content Knowledge and Expertise

**Dimension 2.3:** Communication

**Dimension 2.4:** Differentiation

**Dimension 2.5:** Monitor and Adjust

# Achieving Expectations

*The teacher supports all learners in their pursuit of high levels of academic and social-emotional success.*

Johnny Lingo is the hero in a story about the power of expectations (McGerr, 1988). Born in an area of arranged marriages and dowry requirements, Johnny chose to marry a woman in the village who many felt was unattractive. The woman was shy, and the years of being told she was ugly left her further detached from others in the village. Johnny set the tone of his love for her by offering eight cows for the dowry. This was unheard of, and many in the village felt the father would be lucky to get a tail from a cow. Nevertheless, Johnny brought the cows and took his bride.

He left the village for a period of time, treating his wife like the beauty he saw in her. After a time, he returned to the village with his wife, and everyone was shocked at the gorgeous woman she had become. The father felt robbed, saying she was worth much more than the eight cows he had been given.

The phenomenon, often called the Pygmalion effect, may be seen in schools throughout the country. Teachers who expect high levels of achievement in their students, and simply see students as more capable than they see themselves, often get achievement that is beyond what anyone thought possible.

The average teacher is estimated to make over 3,000 decisions in an average school day (Danielson, 1996), from what activities to teach to when to scratch a lesson and find a new way to teach a concept. Perhaps it is something more trivial, such as whether to go outside or stay inside for recess on a cold day. Teachers are constantly making decisions, and one of the most important is to set high expectations for all students. Dimension 2.1 connects with ways in which the teacher is facilitating the students' own pursuit of success. This dimension requires teachers to establish a learning environment where students are challenged and able to show mastery of learning objectives. All the while, the teacher pushes students to take ownership of their learning. Additionally, teachers must monitor student learning in a way that addresses students' misunderstandings and mistakes.

While proficient teachers set expectations that challenge all students, distinguished teachers push students to set high expectations for themselves. Teachers may do so by having goal-setting meetings where students are taught to set and monitor their own goals for learning.

Teachers should develop an environment where students have the opportunity to set high expectations for themselves and monitor their own social interactions and academic achievement. For example, students might be working on projects in which there is significant autonomy within certain guidelines created by the teacher. This could work on collaborative work, as well. Proficient teachers are good at setting expectations and holding students accountable for getting there. Distinguished teachers have students believe it is all their idea.

Highly effective teachers monitor students' learning to ensure the students are working on goals and setting expectations that are aligned to the course standards. Similarly, teachers must monitor the students' mastery of the content and be prepared to reteach using different instructional methods to ensure all students have mastered the objectives of the lesson.

## A Brief Look at 2.1 in Action

Ms. Miller, a fifth-grade teacher at Parkville Elementary School, called five students to her small-group table as part of a goal-setting process. She asked the students to find their goal-setting sheets. The students briefly reviewed their performance on the previous unit and identified areas that require continued work. Ms. Miller took notes on an electronic form that provided her greater access to the information. Ms. Miller would later use these notes for planning future instruction.

Ms. Miller guided the group of students as they set individualized goals related to the new unit of study. She shared the unit's learning objectives and the pre-assessment data from the previous day's pretest. Each student analyzed his or her results and set goals for the upcoming unit. After all students had set their goals with Ms. Miller's guidance to ensure alignment to the standards, the day's math lesson began.

While students participated in the lesson and completed the required group activities, Ms. Miller monitored for understanding. As she monitored, she noticed that a large number of students were struggling to understand the new concepts. Ms. Miller called the class back and retaught the concept using a different strategy. After providing additional examples and guided practices, she allowed students to go back to their group work. Although the students were working in groups, Ms. Miller recognized some individual students were struggling and checked for understanding. The students expressed their misunderstanding, so Ms. Miller called a small group of students to her table. She provided the students with the opportunity to share what they understood and what they were struggling with (allowing students to self-monitor). Ms. Miller presented the information a different way (persisting with the lesson and looking for evidence that the students are mastering the objective). After the mini-lesson in the small group, the students returned to their groups and continued to work while Ms. Miller monitored for mastery of the standards. To close the day's lesson, Ms. Miller asked students to go back to their goals and make notes about their progress.

Ms. Miller could have chosen to assign group work and address small groups during the lesson, which facilitates and supports all learners in pursuit of academic success. In this case, she was introducing a concept for the first time and chose a whole-group activity. In the following days, she taught a mini-lesson, no more than 10 minutes, at the beginning of the math block and had students transition to math stations where they worked on different activities. She then pulled students to work on differentiated lessons based on the students' academic needs. She always begins and ends the lessons by referring to the students' goals.

As students become more comfortable with setting their own goals for learning, the process only takes a few minutes and can be a whole-group activity. However, the teacher's efforts to monitor the progress should be in a small-group or one-on-one format to ensure student success. The goal-setting sheets can be paper copies or electronic. Google Drive, Office365, or other similar web-based forms facilitate the teacher's monitoring of the process. If paper goal sheets are used, the teacher has to implement a system to monitor the process, such as goal-setting notebooks or a class data display for students to share their goals and chart their progress.

## The Big Three

A good lesson will always fall short of greatness if the instruction has no positive impact on student learning. Teachers must provide opportunities for students to excel while being aware of their struggles, to give them the opportunity to self-correct and truly master the content. In order for students to achieve at high levels of academic and social-emotional success, teachers must:

1. Accept no excuses and set high expectations for all students, regardless of their background or previous academic history. If students know their teachers believe they are capable of being successful and learning at high levels, they will rise to the occasion.
2. Have high expectations, but support students when they struggle. Distinguished teachers go beyond setting high expectations. They do not give up on their students; they persist with the lesson, while using varied strategies, until the students get it.
3. Make goal setting among students an expectation. Students must understand what they must learn, where they are currently, and how to reach their goals. This allows them to monitor their own progress and make adjustments when mistakes are made. Students must take ownership in their learning, their mistakes, and their success.

## Points to Remember

- Students should be given the opportunity to set their own goals and establish expectations for their learning and behavior. However, moving to this level of autonomy takes a plan, and it is a process that will not happen overnight.
- Teachers should find different ways to teach and reteach a concept, without abandoning the lesson, until all students have shown mastery of the objective.
- Students should be taught how to, and be given opportunities to, monitor their progress toward their learning goals, including opportunities to correct their mistakes.
- Each student should be aware of his or her progress on standards. The reason for any tutoring or remediation should not be mysterious to the individual.
- Students from low socioeconomic backgrounds need high expectations more than anyone.

# The Administrative Lens

An administrator evaluating a lesson and looking for evidence that students are achieving expectations should consider:

- Are the students given the opportunity to set academic and behavioral expectations for themselves?
- Is it clear that students are moving toward autonomy and understanding regarding their status on curriculum and socio-emotional standards?
- Are students allowed to self-correct?
- Does the teacher persevere until all students show mastery of the lesson's learning objective?
- What system has the teacher established for students to set goals and monitor their progress toward achieving their goals?

# Moving from Proficient to Distinguished

Supporting students to achieve high levels of success looks significantly different in a proficient lesson than in a distinguished lesson. While in both lessons, the teachers have set high expectations for students and persist with the lesson to ensure student success, proficient teachers move on to the next activity or lesson once most students have mastered the skills. In a distinguished lesson, teachers not only set high expectations, they also push students to set their own goals and expectations for success. Furthermore, teachers continue to work with the students until all students have shown mastery of the content while using various instructional strategies. Teachers in need of ideas on how to ensure all students have mastered the content could benefit from professional development on scaffolding, the gradual release model, and differentiation.

Scaffolding helps students ease into rigorous learning. Through scaffolding teachers can ensure all students are successful by using instructional techniques that progressively move students through the lesson until they have completed it. It is important to note that differentiation and scaffolding are not the same thing. Scaffolding is about breaking up a lesson into smaller chunks and providing strategies or activities for students to master along the way, with the intent that students will master all components of the lesson. Through scaffolding, teachers could also focus on prerequisite skills for an upcoming lesson to address learning gaps before moving on to the focus lesson. Whether used to address learning gaps or to process the lesson, scaffolding provides a structure to help students master the on-level learning objectives. On the other hand, through differentiated learning, teachers modify the lessons based on the students' academic needs, interests, or learning profile, and provide different content, context, or products based on those needs. We'll take a more in-depth look at differentiation in Dimension 2.4.

Understanding the gradual release model would also benefit teachers seeking ways to ensure all students master the standards. Through the use of a gradual release of learning responsibility, teachers model for the students, provide opportunities for students to work under the teachers' guidance, allow students to share the learning responsibility with other students, all before they move into independent practice where every child is responsible for their own learning. Through this process, teachers can move through a lesson while assisting students in monitoring progress. Students who are ready can move on to independent practice while those who are struggling can spend more time in guided practice. The gradual release model allows some students to move on with learning while allowing for additional time for those in need of additional instruction. All three instructional protocols—scaffolding, differentiation, and the gradual release model—provide teachers with tools to support students in their pursuit of high levels of academic and social-emotional success.

Teachers must also understand the importance of providing students with the opportunity to monitor their own learning. During proficient lessons, teachers monitor for misunderstanding and address student mistakes; in a distinguished lesson, the students self-monitor and self-correct their mistakes. Students working with highly effective teachers are aware of their learning and progress and can identify when they are struggling. Students in distinguished classrooms own their learning while the teachers facilitate learning. Teachers looking for ways to improve in this area must spend time teaching students how to monitor their own learning; students are not accustomed to doing so. For years, this responsibility has fallen completely on the teachers' shoulders and students have simply been told if they passed or failed. Additionally, teachers must be committed and spend time creating a learning environment in which the students feel safe to take risks and make mistakes. The teachers' efforts to establish systems for students to monitor their own learning will result in confident, self-reflective students, who are conscious of their goals and their progress toward those goals. This is the outcome to be at the distinguished level.

Danielson, C. (1996). *Enhancing professional practice: A framework for teaching.* Alexandria, VA: Association for Supervision and Curriculum Development. McGerr, P. (1988). The eight-cow wife. *Reader's Digest,* 138–141.

# 2.2

# Content Knowledge and Expertise

*The teacher uses content and pedagogical expertise to design and execute lessons aligned with state standards, related content, and student needs.*

---

Teaching well is more than knowing your discipline; it includes managing and structuring a class in a way that impacts students. However, if you do not know your subject, it becomes apparent during an observation; the instruction can be too complicated and confusing, or perhaps inaccurate. Teachers who know their topic well can provide meaning through simple and clear information, providing examples that illuminate the gaps of understanding found within the students. There are a number of excellent teachers who make complicated material come to life, but one of the best was the late Carl Sagan (Achenbach, 2014).

Carl Sagan was a popularizer of science. He was able to take diverse fields of interest, from biology to astronomy, and develop a deep understanding of the concepts among those that read or heard him. His book *Dragons of Eden* (1977) educated a generation on early earth, and his television series *Cosmos* lit the intellectual fire for future scientists. His approach was interdisciplinary, consistent (check YouTube for his discussions with the late-night host Johnny Carson, another great teacher), and connective with prior learning while being both simple and deep. This is not an easy combination of traits, but one that does exist within most teachers.

Content knowledge is important for an obvious reason: If teachers do not know the discipline, there is nothing to share with students. But content knowledge is not enough to be a great teacher. The T-TESS says that teachers are proficient by accurately conveying knowledge, but distinguished teachers must truly understand it in order to consistently provide students with opportunities to think critically about the content.

Understanding content as a distinguished teacher means being able to connect it with other disciplines. Regardless of the topic, there are ways to incorporate math, science, language arts, history, and just about anything else. Depth of understanding spotlights the interrelatedness of knowledge, and it adds to being able to use that learning in multiple contexts. These contexts may include authentic projects, problem-based learning, creative endeavors, and other assignments that promote different types of thinking. Distinguished lessons, taught by teachers with extensive knowledge of their content, provide students with opportunities to understand how the standards relate to life outside the classroom. Teachers who have a deep understanding of their content and effectively execute strong lessons have a great impact on student learning.

## A Brief Look at 2.2 in Action

Jill Smith, biology teacher at Smithson High School, walks around the lab tables as her students take their seats before the tardy bell. Even before the bell rings, she starts explaining to the class, "Today we are going to continue looking at the processes of the plant, this time discussing the process of photosynthesis." The students copy the objective into their notebooks.

"Yesterday we looked at how water was pulled through the plant. What is the structure that transports water through the plant?" Several students raise hands as she walks by them, but she cold calls a student she is trying to encourage, in part, because she knows he knows the answer. "Detrick, what is that structure?"

"The xylem," he says quietly. He is a shy student, and Mrs. Smith's efforts to slowly pull him out of his shell are paying off. She sees in him a strong leader.

"Excellent," Mrs. Smith says. "Now, heads together," she started with one of her group discussion procedures, "How could you design a water transport system on an island using processes used by the xylem?" She wants to push the students a little deeper into understanding this process. She gives the students a few minutes of discussion and scribbling before continuing the discussion.

After a good class discussion on water systems, she continues to set the stage for the lesson by connecting with previous learning, discussing the chemical processes of photosynthesis, showing why it was important to everyday existence and providing analogous examples from other parts of life. She wants the students to explore with hands-on activities, but this topic needs a clean and clear explanation up front, so the lecture was a little longer than usual as she has anticipated and is addressing possible misunderstandings; nevertheless, she effortlessly has the class move into a lab that separates the pigment of a leaf. The lab takes about 10 minutes to start, and the separation is going to take until the next day.

Mrs. Smith is 25 minutes into class, and she got their attention. "Heads up, everyone. I want you to work within your lab group and answer the question on the whiteboard. You have 3 minutes." The question that requires a deeper level of knowledge while exposing the students to the End of Course standardized test format. She wants to see the students work through a photosynthesis question collaboratively. She saves her difficult questions for groups, using slightly more rigorous ones than those used for individual assessment.

Once the time was up, Mrs. Smith checks answers and debriefs the question with students. She is 31 minutes into her 50-minute class. She transitions into a new assignment.

"Ms. Evans mentioned you guys are reading *The Good Earth* in English. I have an excerpt of the novel in the assignment section of your lab table. Take it out, read it, and be prepared to share your thoughts about the following: The novel is set early in the twentieth century. How do problems the farmers faced then compare to issues that farmers face nowadays? Be ready to support your answer with the scientific information we have discussed in this course." The students dig into the work while helping them prepare for their next class.

# The Big Three

Regardless of the class level or subject, the expectations set forth in Dimension 2.2 require that teachers have a deep understanding of their lessons and the ability to connect it to other disciplines. Their understanding of the subjects must be strong enough for the teachers to be able to the following:

1. Anticipate common misunderstandings and take the necessary measures to address those throughout the lesson in order to help students have an accurate understanding of the content.

2. Avoid teaching the content in isolation. The sequence of the lesson and the activities should allow students to understand how the content not only relates to other units within the course but to other subjects, and most importantly, to the real world.

3. Plan and teach lessons that guarantee students have a strong understanding of the content while given the opportunity to apply and think critically about the topic. Understanding the depth of knowledge required of the standards is very important to ensure that the activities and questions that students are exposed to are at the appropriate level of thinking. By ensuring alignment of lessons to the depth of knowledge of the TEKS, teachers responsible for STAAR/EOC subjects ensure that their instruction connects to the rigor of the state tests.

## Points to Remember

- Accuracy is imperative. Failure to explain a concept according to the best understanding of the discipline is a sure way to be considered "improvement needed."
- Connecting the topic to other disciplines is a sign of a distinguished teacher.
- Help students understand why learning the content is relevant to life outside the classroom.
- Regardless of the complexity of the content, students have to be given the opportunity to think critically and problem solve. Avoid teaching knowledge and skills in isolation.
- The teachers' deep understanding of the content will facilitate the design and teaching of lessons that are adequately sequenced.
- During the planning phase, consider the common misconceptions students have about the content and be ready to address those. Be proactive.

## The Administrative Lens

An administrator conducting an observation and collecting evidence to rate this dimension should consider:

- Is the concept aligned with the TEKS content, cognitive, and context expectations?
- How did the sequence of the lesson impact student learning?
- Is the concept used in multiple contexts?
- Are students given the opportunity to apply the content to real-life situations?
- Does the teacher know what is being taught? Was this evident through instructional clarity?
- Were students experiencing success with the academic concept?
- Did the teacher anticipate misconceptions? If so, how were those misconceptions addressed to ensure students have an accurate understanding of the content?
- What type of opportunities did the teacher provide for the students to think critically?

## Moving from Proficient to Distinguished

All teachers have a favorite subject that they love to teach, but that does not preclude them from teaching other topics in depth. After all, school principals must assign teachers who are certified to teach certain subjects or grade levels based on student enrollment and personnel allocations. Teachers must have the same depth of knowledge about all the subjects they teach, whether they love the content or simply teach it because they have to. Proficient teachers have a basic, accurate understanding of the discipline but a lack of understanding prevents them from teaching the content to the specificity and complexity that it requires. Distinguished teachers have a deep understanding of content knowledge, and it is evident in their teaching. They can help students understand complex concepts while making it all seem simple. All teachers must make the commitment to become experts in the subject they teach.

Teachers who need a better understanding of the content have multiple resources within their reach. First, teachers can rely on their colleagues who teach the same content areas by engaging in conversations with these local experts, and through this can expand their understanding of the discipline and best practices to teach it. Teachers that work in small schools or districts where they might be the only teacher responsible for that subject should reach out to colleagues in neighboring campuses, or contact the content coordinators at the Educational Service Center (ESC). Contacts at the ESC would be able to provide direction on workshops focused on content.

On the other side of the spectrum, some teachers might have a strong understanding of their content but lack instructional expertise. Having expertise in a content area does not guarantee the teachers will present distinguished lessons. The lessons must be adequately sequenced while providing students with accurate content and opportunities to engage in rigorous learning. Teachers with a strong understanding of their content who need to expand their repertoire of instructional strategies should focus on learning about best instructional practices for that discipline. In addition to attending professional development, there are many model lessons available online for teachers to watch and learn from, and there might be distinguished teachers on campus willing to work with those in need of ideas to improve their delivery of instruction.

Achenbach, J. (2014, March). Why Carl Sagan is truly irreplaceable. *Smithsonian Magazine*. Retrieved from http://www.smithsonianmag.com/science-nature/why-carl-sagan-truly-irreplaceable-180949818/?no-ist
Sagan, C. (1977). *The dragons of Eden*. New York, NY: Random House.

# Communication

*The teacher clearly and accurately communicates to support persistence, deeper learning, and effective effort.*

Communication in classrooms is wrapped around high expectations from the teachers and mutual respect for all. Anyone who has observed teachers is able to feel this immediately upon watching the lessons. It is more than compliance and obedience; distinguished classrooms have the feel of enjoyment and exploration. Teachers model appropriate verbal and written communication while expecting the same from the students as they interact with their peers. Distinguished teachers leverage effective communication practices to address misconceptions while encouraging student perseverance to succeed in learning. The practices established in these classrooms promote a risk-free environment for deeper learning.

A big part of Dimension 2.3 is the way in which teachers are using questioning strategies in their lessons, but for these efforts to work well, classrooms must be places where the students feel safe. Pushing students to think more deeply through questioning forces them to take chances with their answers. A classroom in which students support one another and are unafraid to intellectually explore is a prerequisite to doing well in regard to communication. That being said, effective questioning strategies are often lacking in teachers' repertoire.

Effective questioning requires teachers to do something that feels unnatural—that is, slow down and give students the time to work through a problem while providing prompts and minimal guidance. Questioning forces teachers to not provide the answer but requires students to use the rational skills they need to develop. Furthermore, students have to be given opportunities to ask questions and engage in academic conversations. By modeling how to ask questions at high levels of thinking, teachers are providing students with examples and ways to elicit higher-order thinking, but ultimately, students should be driving their own learning by posing questions and having student-led conversations.

The classic questioning strategy, taught in every school of education in the nation, is Bloom's taxonomy. In the revised Bloom's, there are six levels of questioning:

1. Remembering
2. Understanding
3. Applying
4. Analyzing
5. Evaluating
6. Creating

The list shows the order of higher-level questions, with creating ones being the highest. A national study sponsored by the U.S. Department of Education reported that only 20% of the questions K-12 teachers ask are at the higher cognitive levels (Cotton, n.d.); students are consistently asked questions at the remembering and understanding levels. However, distinguished teachers constantly ask, and their students generate, questions at the highest cognitive levels.

The problems with questioning are that (1) teachers often neglect to ask anything but the most basic questions that students can answer by recalling information, and (2) students are not given the opportunity to drive their learning by asking questions. These common practices result in learning at lower cognitive levels, which limits the effectiveness of the lessons.

A study among college students found that teachers rarely asked questions that required depth of analysis, and even then there were many questions that were not answered. Part of the problem was wait time, as instructors often got impatient. The average wait-time requirement to get an answer was 5 seconds (Larson & Lovelace, 2013). Five seconds of silence can be difficult.

Questioning often comes down to implementing the preparation. Plan for questions that get students to mentally explore the concept in different ways; plan activities that allow students time to generate their own questions. Try to get them excited by asking questions that relate to their interests. Open-ended questions are best, requiring greater understanding of the concept to provide an answer; and an open-ended question allows the teacher to formatively assess understanding.

These questions are still teacher produced, and one of the T-TESS objectives is for the student to take ownership of his or her learning. Rothstein, Santana, and Minigan (2015) have formulated a student-based questioning process called the Question Formulation Technique (QFT). The QFT has students create questions related to the standard being taught. The process is simple (the best strategies are) and includes brainstorming questions in a safe environment, slowly working with students to help them ask better questions, and having them explore the answers.

# A Brief Look at 2.3 in Action

Sam Gibbons took it as a point of pride that his students often asked questions that were too complicated for him to answer on the spot. This was the point, he thought. Students, when younger, came up with questions about the world that were unanswerable. He wanted his sophomore biology students to regain that curiosity. And then he wanted them to find the answer.

The students were working in lab groups. He put these groups into place based on particular skills of each student-member, and the purpose of this arrangement today was to get better questions from the group. They were working on the nervous system, having just completed a simulation showing the passing of electrical currents through nerves.

"In looking at the processes within the nervous system, what does this make you question?" Mr. Gibbons asked. The class knew the procedures and began to discuss and brainstorm questions in their groups.

At this point, everyone was accustomed to the process and felt comfortable asking anything. Why did the nervous system evolve? What would happen if an individual did not have nerves? What would a nervous system look like on a different planet? And so on. Mr. Gibbons continued to prompt the group to think deeper, and he had the laptops accessible for the next part of the lab, which would require a further look at the questions created by the students.

# The Big Three

Establishing a classroom environment where students feel safe is key to the execution of distinguished lessons. Teachers must clearly communicate with students, but in distinguished classrooms there is also evidence of academic communication among students. As teachers, make sure you address the top three characteristics:

1. Set clear expectations and put procedures in place that promote risk taking. This means that students need to feel emotionally safe to say things that may end up being silly. Model appropriate communication so once the students start to take risks, they do so in a respectful and appropriate way.
2. Practice good questioning. Many teachers have an idea of what needs to be done, but it sometimes feels unnatural. Take the time to learn about a best practice in this realm, and practice it.
3. Push questioning onto students. Distinguished teachers have classrooms where students take ownership of their learning, lead the academic conversations, and one of the steps is getting them to ask good questions.

# Points to Remember

- Students need to feel emotionally safe for questioning to be effective. Students may be concerned that their responses (or questions) will be ridiculed by their peers. A culture of acceptance is important for the classroom.
- Plan questions that require critical thinking for lessons, and anticipate misconceptions so you're prepared to clarify mistakes.
- The questions should not only promote higher order thinking but also lead students to engage in academic conversations.
- Have students create their own questions, and have high expectations that the student-generated queries will be intellectually deep. Keep prompting students to ask better questions.
- Practice good questioning techniques: higher-level questions, good wait time, prompting, etc.
- Build on content knowledge, which will add to questioning skills.
- Do not always answer student questions; have them explore and hypothesize to get the answer.
- Balance question exploration with time factors.

# The Administrative Lens

When scripting a lesson or observing a classroom, look for evidence for these questions:

- What opportunities does the teacher provide for students to communicate with their peers about learning?
- Does the teacher ask questions at the application, creative, or evaluative level?
- Does the teacher use other questioning strategies, such as wait time, effectively?
- What are the classroom expectations regarding students developing their own questions?
- Does the teacher prompt students to explore in greater depth?
- Does the teacher anticipate areas of lesson difficulty and use this confusion as a step to explore more deeply?
- Is the classroom emotionally safe?

# Moving from Proficient to Distinguished

Teachers are comfortable with leading the classroom and conveying information, but questioning and allowing students to take ownership of their learning are often areas of difficulty. Dimension 2.3 requires that the classroom be conducive to conversations and exploration while turning over portions of class time to students, and these expectations do not come naturally to many educators.

Proficient teachers provide some opportunities for peer communication while distinguished teachers establish classrooms and teach lessons in which all students feel safe participating, sharing, and asking questions. For teachers to move from proficient to distinguished, they must establish a safe learning environment while modeling how to have academic conversations and ask questions.

Moving from proficient to distinguished also requires learning more about questioning and practicing it on a daily basis. Prompting, wait time, and higher-level questions are all communication characteristics of distinguished teachers. Students who are consistently required to answer higher-level questions begin to think about the work being done at a deeper level. Teachers interested in distinguished lessons should plan the questions they will ask ahead of time and anticipate students' misconceptions about the subject. They must take the time to expand their understanding of Bloom's taxonomy.

In addition to focusing on Bloom's taxonomy, teachers must also understand the depth of knowledge expected of the standards. Dr. Norman Webb's Depth of Knowledge (DOK) encourages teachers to analyze all questions and tasks to identify their cognitive expectations. While Bloom's taxonomy gives teachers a starting point, the DOK level goes beyond the verb. DOK requires teachers to think about the context and the level of understanding the question or task requires of the students. The level of Bloom's of the questions should be used in conjunction with the context in which the learning takes place, or the DOK, to ensure that the students are working in alignment to the cognitive expectations of the TEKS. Understanding the depth of knowledge and cognitive expectations of the TEKS will facilitate the planning and execution of distinguished lessons.

The T-TESS is about student-centered learning by pushing more responsibility onto students. Distinguished teachers expect students to ask the questions, not just answer them. There will be occasional modeling and regular prompting, but getting students to question work will increase the level of ownership they feel for it. It will pique the students' curiosity and increase the cognitive expectations of the lessons.

Cotton, K. (n.d.). *Classroom questioning.* Retrieved from https://www.learner.org/workshops/socialstudies/pdf/session/6.ClassroomQuestioning.pdf

Larson, L. R., & Lovelace, M. D. (2013). Evaluating the efficacy of questioning strategies in lecture-based classroom environments: Are we asking the right questions? *Journal on Excellence in College Teaching, 24*(1), 105–122.

Rothstein, D., Santana, L., & Minigan, A. P. (2015). Making questions flow. *Educational Leadership, 73*(1), 70–75.

# 2.4

# Differentiation

*The teacher differentiates instruction, aligning methods and techniques to diverse student needs.*

---

A lesson that teaches at the level in which the standards were written with no consideration for students' readiness, interests, and learning styles will be of limited effectiveness. If a lesson is to meet the needs of the students, instruction has to be differentiated. Differentiation is the process through which teachers design lessons that address students' academic needs, interests, and learning styles. Through differentiation, the teacher can adapt the content of the activities, the process through which the students access the curriculum, or the product through which the students show mastery of the standards. By designing lessons that take needs, interests, and/or learning styles into consideration, teachers increase student engagement in learning.

The use of assessment data facilitates the design of differentiated instruction based on student readiness. For instance, reading teachers that are aware of their students' reading levels can design lessons using text at various levels, differentiating the content of the lesson based on student readiness. At the same time, teachers can differentiate the learning process by using learning strategies to teach the same concepts based on the students' reading levels. Furthermore, if students in that reading group are expected to demonstrate mastery of the standards by completing a different activity, teachers may differentiate the product based on student readiness.

Science teachers can differentiate learning based on students' interests by allowing for choice when designing research projects. For example, in a biology classroom students might be expected to complete a DNA research project that will assess the set of standards. By giving students the opportunity to choose the species they will research, teachers differentiate the learning based on students' interests. During that same unit, students might have access to a variety of resources, such as books, magazines, web-based resources, videos, and teachers' mini-lessons. By providing a variety of standards-based resources, the teacher is addressing the students' varied learning styles. It is critical that when teachers are designing differentiated learning based on the students' interests or learning styles, they have to set clear expectations to ensure learning is closely aligned to the standards.

Furthermore, teachers must put in place systems to monitor learning to ensure all students are working toward mastery of the standards at the cognitive level in which the standards were written. While differentiating is key to the success of all students, when learning is differentiated based on readiness, teachers must design lessons that ensure that struggling students are moving toward on-level work.

## A Brief Look at 2.4 in Action

Jennifer Johnson had the reputation for knowing more about her students than anyone else in the school, and she wanted to keep it that way. She used a variety of assessment techniques, many informal, but others required students to show an understanding of the knowledge and skills in multiple contexts. Ms. Johnson had a system in place to record her students' progress, strengths, and weaknesses as measured by the various assessments, which she used in planning her lessons. She purposefully built rapport with the students so she knew what was interesting to each one of them. Her efforts paid off, because her data and knowledge of students allowed her to target certain activities to the students' personal preferences.

Prior to this math lesson, Ms. Johnson had assessed her students' understanding of angles and the relationship between lengths of sides and measures of angles in a triangle. She used the pre-assessment data and her knowledge of students to design differentiated instruction based on student readiness. On the day of the lesson, after she stated the objective for the day and presented a whole-group mini-lesson, students were divided into three groups: (1) students who needed to strengthen the prerequisite skills, (2) those who have the skills and are academically ready for the on-level activities, and (3) students who have mastered the day's objective and would benefit from enrichment activities. Each of the activities are different not only based on student readiness, but Ms. Johnson gave students a choice in the product they'll create to demonstrate mastery of the content. She provided clear guidelines to make sure the products the students created were closely aligned to the standards.

Students worked in small groups while Ms. Johnson walked around the room assessing for understanding. She also pulled struggling students and worked with them to reteach using different instructional strategies. It is important to note that once students in the prerequisite skills group demonstrated mastery, they were assigned the on-level activity. Although Ms. Johnson differentiated based on readiness and provided activities for struggling students that were below grade level, her expectation for all students was that they master the on-level standards.

# The Big Three

Effective differentiation requires a strong knowledge of students, as well as instructional creativity to meet the various needs. The big picture includes the following:

1.  Differentiation is where data and knowledge of students come together. Setting up instruction to address gaps in knowledge or skills in personal yet meaningful ways can be difficult. Not every student is motivated by the same activity, nor do they all process new information the same way. Develop a creative classroom that consistently measures the effectiveness of instruction in increasing engagement and achievement.
2.  Differentiated instruction requires procedures and routines to be in place in order to be effective. Prepare students early in the year to transition to new activities, work in groups, show support, and maintain focus while teachers monitor for understanding and facilitate learning. Student-directed learning will make differentiation much easier to manage.
3.  Student engagement becomes more effective when differentiated activities align with the students' life or interests. There may be some instruction that is seemingly removed from the life of our students, but try to connect it when possible.

# Points to Remember

- Differentiation is more than just presenting the content using various teaching techniques; it includes targeted and purposeful instruction based on the needs of both individuals and groups.
- It requires teachers that are aware of their students' progress and quality of performance so they can adapt the instruction to ensure students are engaged in learning.
- Teachers can differentiate the content, process, and product based on readiness, interests, or learning styles.
- While differentiation helps struggling students access the curriculum, the goal should be to scaffold instruction to ensure they are able to access the on-level curriculum, but don't confuse scaffolding with differentiation!
- Differentiation is not just for struggling students; some students need enrichment activities because they have already mastered the content of the unit. By differentiating their instruction, they can stay cognitively engaged in learning.
- By differentiating learning, teachers increase student engagement by allowing students the opportunity to participate in activities that are at their learning level, or by addressing their interest or learning styles.

# The Administrative Lens

An administrator needs to look for evidence of the following:

- Is the teacher monitoring the students' work and behavior?
- How is the teacher using observational and assessment data to adapt instruction to meet the academic needs of the students?
- Are the students engaged in multiple instructional activities?
- Are activities aligned with student interest and needs?
- Does the differentiation target the needs of individual students?
- Do the students understand the knowledge and skills in multiple contexts?
- Do the procedures and routines support differentiated learning by providing greater efficiency and emotional safety?

# Moving from Proficient to Distinguished

In order to implement differentiated instruction, teachers must have a deep understanding of the standards, their students, and instructional practices. Teachers must have a deep understanding of the standards so they can plan activities that provide students with opportunities to learn and apply the content and skills of standards in multiple contexts. By providing activities in which students apply the knowledge in multiple ways, teachers ensure that the students are able to recognize how a standard fits within different contexts. Teachers should plan varied activities that are closely aligned to the standards while addressing the students' needs, interests, and learning styles; it is not an easy task but one that is doable when the teachers possess a deep understanding of the content and their students.

When teachers have the required understanding of the standards, they can provide differentiated instruction for individual students based upon needs. Coaches do this all the time in practice, requiring running backs to work on different drills than linemen. The coaching situation seems obvious; the players need to get better with different skills. The same is true within our classrooms.

All concepts of differentiation require a teacher who understands multiple ways to teach a subject, as well as understanding of the prerequisite skills needed to master it. Teachers moving toward the distinguished level are going to need an instructional toolbox that keeps growing to accommodate new classroom challenges, including varied levels of academic readiness and an infinite number of student interests. Take advantage of books and professional development sessions that provide practical solutions to differentiation. Furthermore, when planning with your team, do not forget to rely on your colleagues who might have different ideas to teach the same knowledge and skills. Take the opportunity to understand how to better address students' learning gaps through differentiated instruction.

Differentiation, in order to be effective, requires that teachers be strong in many other dimensions. Planning allows for the use of multiple instructional strategies, data are needed to recognize needs for both individuals and groups, strong procedures provide the foundation for movement and risk taking within the activities, and expectations set the tone for the behavior and level of achievement. A distinguished teacher in this dimension will need to be accomplished in these other areas; otherwise, any differentiated instructional strategy will appear poor. Many of the other dimensions will need to set the foundation for effective differentiation.

# Monitor
# and Adjust

*The teacher formally and informally collects, analyzes, and uses student progress data and makes needed lesson adjustments.*

Teachers go into their classrooms determined to do their best and reach every child. They have spent countless hours preparing for the day's lessons and understand the challenges their students will face as they tackle new knowledge and skills. However, the success of those lessons goes beyond a solid plan and successful execution of direct teaching. Distinguished teachers understand their students' needs and have a system in place to monitor their students' learning and mastery of the content. Teachers' efforts to monitor and adjust the instruction to ensure student learning are key to success. During distinguished lessons, there is ample evidence that students are successful because of the teachers' actions and awareness of the students' needs. Proficient lessons monitor and adjust instruction to ensure students are engaged in learning. In distinguished lessons, the teachers not only invite student input to monitor their understanding, but there are also systems in place to gather evidence and utilize that data to adjust the lesson, the pacing, and the instruction. Teachers that have distinguished lessons are aware of the varied needs of their students and are able to adjust to meet them. For instance, adjustments needed for struggling students are significantly different than those for advanced students, but both are equally important.

By consistently monitoring student learning, teachers can maintain high levels of student engagement. Furthermore, teachers who develop distinguished lessons not only have systems in place to monitor engagement, they ask questions to check for understanding and maximize the opportunities to provide meaningful feedback. By systematically collecting data through questioning, distinguished teachers can pace the lesson and successfully adjust instruction. Furthermore, they provide meaningful feedback to students in order to facilitate content mastery.

Monitoring and adjusting goes beyond walking around the classroom to make sure students are on task. It is about using the student observation data and the students' input to modify the lesson so all students are successful. It is not about repeating the instructions or re-teaching the same lesson; it is about finding a different way to re-teach when there is evidence that the students did not previously grasp the concept. It is about providing additional time when there is evidence that the students need additional time to successfully complete the task, or perhaps, completely discarding the lesson and starting over. Teachers who teach distinguished lessons are aware of their students' needs and the impact their teaching has on learning. Effective monitoring and adjusting of instruction ensures that the teacher's actions have a positive impact on students' learning the lesson's objectives.

## A Brief Look at 2.5 in Action

Ms. Jagger finished teaching a short whole-group review lesson on equivalent fractions to her fifth graders. She has assigned independent practice to a number of students who have demonstrated mastery of the concept. She calls on a small group to check for understanding given their struggles during the whole-group lesson. Ms. Jagger guides students as they solve a number of word problems. After guiding the small group, she walks around the room and engages students in conversation about the work. She notices that two of the students working independently have already completed the assignments. Ms. Jagger has prepared for these advanced students and assigns them a collaborative assignment where they will design a product of their choosing using equivalent fractions. She gives clear expectations of the components that must be included in the fraction to ensure the product is aligned to the standards. By doing so, she has successfully adjusted instruction for the advanced students; not only did she adjust the assignment but modified the pacing of the lesson to ensure students were consistently engaged in learning.

Additionally, when monitoring for understanding, she identified a small group of students who needed additional support. She pulled fraction bars and briefly retaught equivalent fractions to the students using the word problems they were working on. The students who continued to show confusion were pulled to her table while others that understood the instruction were allowed to continue to work independently. The struggling students joined Ms. Jagger for a different mini-lesson on skills needed to master equivalent fractions. After she provided additional instruction, she increased the academic rigor to ensure the students were mastering the content at the level of the standards. By working separately with the small group of students who were still struggling, Ms. Jagger adjusted the instruction. She did not allow students who had previously showed some understanding to struggle when the task became too difficult for them. She consistently monitored and was aware of the needs of her students. Not only did she assess the understanding, but she used the information to adjust the lesson and ensure student success. It is important to note that by adjusting the instruction she ensured that her instruction had a positive impact on student learning.

## The Big Three

Educators that recognize issues in a classroom and adjust to them are more effective at increasing student achievement. Confusion is an enemy of achievement, so recognizing gaps early provides long-term benefits. That being said, monitoring is a big part of this dimension. This leads off our big three:

1. Proximity to students, an important factor for several of the dimensions, is vital here, as well. Being close to students and commenting on their work sends a message that what they are doing matters. This will help get the students' best work, so the teacher will actually get a better understanding if difficulty is due to understanding or effort. Furthermore, proximity allows the teacher to see errors early and provide on-the-spot interventions.
2. A good understanding of the content allows the instructor to predict areas of misunderstanding. Paying particular attention to these difficult concepts allows for more reinforcement and predictable adjustments as monitoring occurs.
3. Learn more about instructional strategies that you do not typically use. This builds on the professional repertoire needed to be able to modify instruction more effectively.

## Points to Remember

- Distinguished teachers put systems in place that facilitate the monitoring of student learning.
- Use the collected information to adapt instruction and/or the pacing of the lesson to ensure student success.
- Develop formative evaluation methods that are subtle and discreet.
- If there is evidence that the students have mastered the learning objectives, provide enrichment activities.
- If there is evidence that the students are struggling, reteach using different instructional strategies and adjust the pacing of the lesson.

## The Administrative Lens

An administrator needs to look for evidence of the following:

- As the lesson progresses, is the teacher checking for understanding?
- Is the teacher using data to help plan the lesson?
- Is the teacher in proximity to the students, thus allowing for effective monitoring?
- How is the teacher using the information gathered to adjust the lesson to make sure students are mastering the learning objectives?
- When the teacher adjusts the lesson, is the teacher using different instructional strategies to reteach?

## Moving from Proficient to Distinguished

The ability to monitor and adjust well is important in addressing learning gaps before they get too big. The ability to do this is contingent upon plans on how to formatively evaluate the students' understanding of the knowledge and skills being taught. There is a clear connection of this dimension to the questioning in Dimension 2.3. Questions need to be of sufficient depth to provide evidence that students understand the concept properly, and proximity monitoring needs to support increased clarity of student understanding.

Student understanding of any standard must be shown in multiple contexts, which aligns with differentiation. For teachers who teach a subject tested through STAAR/EOC, this includes objective multiple-choice questions. Therefore, a teacher in these tested subjects must make the STAAR/EOC format one of the contexts in which the students express their understanding of the lesson.

Moving to the distinguished level requires a strong understanding of the status of each student, as well as the expertise to adjust lessons to address any difficulties. Experienced teachers who regularly monitor and adjust are able to do so quietly and unobtrusively. Learn to recognize potential problems quickly, and practice addressing them. Experience is a great teacher, but being distinguished can be expedited through professional development in formative assessments.

# Learning Environment

**Dimension 3.1:** Classroom Environment, Routines, and Procedures

**Dimension 3.2:** Managing Student Behavior

**Dimension 3.3:** Classroom Culture

# Classroom Environment, Routines, and Procedures

*The teacher organizes a safe, accessible and efficient classroom.*

Harry and Rosemary Wong (2009), in their classic book *The First Days of School*, provide a strong case for clear routines and procedures within the classroom. Teachers who purposefully greet students at the door, assign groups, develop routines for day-to-day functioning, and communicate with parents will have well-managed classrooms. The key is purpose.

Ineffective teachers leave too much to chance. Seating is random, groups are created by students and based on popularity, and transitions are spontaneous. Effective teachers have plans for the classroom environment. Although Dimension 3 is based upon evidence witnessed during the lesson, and may include some pre-conference information, good teachers plan for success. A great classroom environment is thoughtful and strategic.

Teaching is one of the most rewarding jobs a person can have. Developing students to reach high levels of attainment both socially and academically helps create the foundation for lifelong success. In fact, many would argue that teachers have a moral purpose in developing students for a future civic, professional, and personal life. But this moral purpose is unattainable without an organized classroom with efficient procedures.

These procedures are the heart of classroom management. Poorly managed classrooms cannot be effective, and the teachers who create these classrooms will hate their job. The moral purpose of education disappears when teachers dread walking into their classrooms every day due to the lack of control.

A chaotic classroom is not contingent upon the students. As administrators know, the same group of students acts completely different depending upon the teacher. Students who are time wasters and troublemakers will excel in a structured environment.

There are numerous ways to create a classroom with effective and efficient routines and procedures. Here is some general advice:

- Plan … and pay attention to details.
- Ask advice from teachers who are great at managing classes.
- Recognize that procedures that do not work can be changed.
- Strive for continual improvement until the procedures are effective and efficient.
- Realize that it is a process that will not change overnight.
- By assigning students roles, the responsibility of establishing a structured classroom is shared between teachers and students.
- Hold students accountable for their actions and allow them to take increased ownership of their classroom.

# A Brief Look at 3.1 in Action

Lindsay Dreyer, third-grade teacher, was known for her well-organized classrooms. She had students who had been taught in such a way that there were efficient transitions, understood roles, and classroom-wide support that extended from teacher–student to student–student. This was not an accident.

Lindsay began developing this behavior, making it automatic and expected, from the first day of school. Students practiced desired behavior from the first minute of the first day of school. There was no wasted time, and to ensure that this was continued, a chart on the wall showed student efficiency. The students took pride in their efficiency and quietly self-monitored. Lindsay joked to close colleagues that her goal was to make her presence obsolete. Substitute teachers loved being assigned to her classroom because of the ownership the students had taken in their own learning. The students successfully went through the instructional day in her absence.

The principal was aware of Lindsay's organization skills and general reputation prior to his appraisal. Nevertheless, he was impressed. Students began working on an introductory assignment without being prompted, and each group looked to a place on the whiteboard to determine whether they were in the preset groups or working individually, and if in groups, the role for each student within the team.

As the lesson continued, there were several transitions, and students moved quickly to new activities. The transitory signals were subtle, but the students clearly understood their responsibility in the lesson. The principal joked in the post-conference that the lesson looked rehearsed, and Lindsay said that it clearly was. "We have done the same thing with every lesson since day one. I would admit to it being rehearsed," she said. The structures in Lindsey's classroom facilitated rigorous learning while maximizing learning time; the time spent from the beginning of school establishing routines and expectations paid off.

## The Big Three

Developing a strong classroom environment, routines, and procedures does not happen accidentally, and this may be one of the most important areas for professional satisfaction. Remember the big three:

1. The start of school is when students begin to develop their understanding of expectations. Be sure the tone is set on the first day.
2. Pay attention to detail. Effective teachers know that purposeful routines and procedures lead to a good classroom environment.
3. This dimension has similar outcomes as the others—students taking ownership of their own learning. Routines and procedures should be meaningfully embedded into the classroom to the point that they become automatic.

## Points to Remember

- Develop routines and procedures in the classroom that become automatic and put as much responsibility on the students as is developmentally appropriate.
- Find ways to challenge the students to increase efficiency of procedures.

- Have the routines and procedures lead toward more student autonomy.
- Students should learn to be mutually supportive.
- Students should feel safe to experiment and fail.
- The structure should lead to higher-level thinking.

## The Administrative Lens

An administrator evaluating a teacher should consider:

- What systems were in place to provide for efficient and effective procedures and routines?
- Are students leaders within the classroom?
- Do students respect each other and hold each other accountable?
- What actions did the teacher take to ensure that the students understand procedural expectations and execute them effortlessly?
- Is student behavior conducive to learning?
- Do students feel safe to speak and participate in activities?
- Do students support their peers?

## Moving from Proficient to Distinguished

Developing a classroom environment through the management of procedures and routines is vital for proficient performance effectiveness. The rubric calls for "clear and efficient" routines, active engagement, and a safe and orderly environment. Classrooms that have this environment are going to be very good, but they will not be distinguished.

Distinguished classrooms put the responsibility of efficient transitions on the students. This requires consistent pushing on the part of strong teachers who know how to motivate and encourage students. Student autonomy does not come without responsibility, so teachers will continue to push the students toward higher achievement, both socially and academically.

Teachers moving toward a distinguished classroom environment will recognize that this is a process, and thus the students will be subject to developmentally appropriate cues. Early on, the teachers may have to be heavily involved in the procedures, talking through transitions and expectations. Through practice and challenges, students get more efficient, and teachers give progressively more responsibility to the students.

Teachers working to move from proficient to distinguished should reflect on their practices to identify when and where procedures are not aligned with the expectations of the distinguished level. Additionally, teachers should ask to observe a teacher who has successfully established classrooms where students "run the classroom." Seeing a student-driven classroom may provide insight into what it takes to create this environment. It will be important for the teachers to engage in conversation in which the observing teachers have the opportunity to ask questions. Distinguished teachers in this dimension are generally purposeful and can explicitly explain the expectations and systems that have resulted in the creation of student-led classrooms.

Wong, H. K., & Wong, R. T. (2009). *The first days of school: How to be an effective teacher*. Mountain View, CA: Harry K. Wong Publications, Inc.

# 3.2

## Managing
## Student Behavior

*The teacher establishes, communicates and maintains clear expectations for student behavior.*

Establishing a classroom environment conducive to learning goes beyond planning strong lessons and designing a well thought-out classroom management plan. Teachers must set clear expectations and consistently monitor student behavior to facilitate the establishment of an environment conducive to learning. Monitoring student behavior is not just about determining which students are following the rules; distinguished teachers consistently reinforce positive behavior so students are aware and continue to exhibit the behavior. They also redirect misbehavior without interrupting learning. For a classroom management plan to be successfully implemented, teachers must share the responsibility with students.

Students must be held accountable for their behavior but they must also self-monitor and self-direct. When students take ownership of classroom management, they work with the teacher to develop the plan, and most importantly, to monitor their behavior. A simple, clearly understood shared plan must be in place.

Because a classroom discipline plan will be developed with student input, one cannot be listed here. But there are some guidelines to follow:

- The implementation of a plan should be as unobtrusive as possible. A teacher needs to protect instructional time.
- The plan must protect the well-being of the students. Corporal punishment is still allowed in many regions of Texas, but few teachers use it. Protecting students goes beyond excessive force, however; it includes making sure that emotional factors are not compromised.
- The plan must be fairly and consistently implemented.
- The plan must include parent communication.
- The plan needs to have stages that increase consequences for any ongoing misbehavior.
- The principal needs to know the behavior plan and support it.

A teacher–student mutually developed plan that gets parents and the principal involved will get increased support from everyone. Parents want to know if there are problems in the classroom, the principal likes being aware of any disciplinary steps that have occurred prior to a student arriving in his or her office, and students value having a say in the process.

## A Brief Look at 3.2 in Action

Glenda Reed had her technology applications class working independently on an assignment related to webpage development. The students were working on laptops and completing work that allowed creative development of an online marketing site for each student's favorite restaurant. The students had explored several models of landing pages online and brainstormed creative solutions in groups before the independent work. There were good ideas being developed, but as always, students regularly got stuck both creatively and technically. Ms. Reed has a procedure in place where the students ask a peer for assistance before her. As she walks around the room and sees the occasional student getting off track, or creating a product that lacks depth, she tells the student to discuss the issue with a friend.

"David, Charles. You are doing great with the webpage, but let's think a little more about it. What can you add to it to get more customers? Heads together and discuss." David and Charles moved next to each other and began to create new components to the page. David said something that made Charles punch him lightly in the arm. Ms. Reed stared down the two young men, and they immediately got back to work.

She continued to walk around the room and prompt the students to be more creative. Increasing creativity meant the students needed to have better technical skills to be able to create the product. Occasionally, a student would lose focus on the task, but she was always close to the students and would subtly direct them back to their work.

## The Big Three

When working to establish a student behavior management plan, keep in mind these three ideas:

1. Involve students in the development of behavior expectations and the systems you'll use to maintain those standards. Establish routines that will not interfere with teaching and learning.
2. It is not your sole responsibility to manage behavior—expect students to monitor their own behavior.
3. It is as important to reinforce positive behavior as it is to redirect misbehavior. Reinforcing positive behavior encourages students to continue exhibiting the desired behaviors.

## Points to Remember

- The students should be involved in the development of the classroom management plan, including standards for behavior.
- Teachers and students should monitor implementation of the behavior plans.
- The teachers should subtly reinforce appropriate behavior and address misbehavior so the teachers' actions do not interrupt instruction.
- An effective behavior plan allows students to self-monitor and self-direct their behavior.
- Include in the plan a step that makes parents aware of any classroom difficulties involving their child.
- Make sure the principal is supportive of the plan.

## The Administrative Lens

When observing a lesson, look for evidence that answers the following questions:

- Are the teacher's efforts to manage behavior subtle?

- Do the teacher's actions flow with the lesson and not interfere with learning?
- In what ways does the teacher reinforce positive behavior?
- Are students allowed to self-monitor and self-direct their behavior?
- Is there evidence (perhaps in the preconference) that the teacher communicates misbehavior with parents?
- Did the teacher share the plan with the principal early in the year?

## Moving from Proficient to Distinguished

A teacher who is respected by students rarely has to work hard at managing student behavior. Respect is a result of consistent preparedness, high professionalism, and overall caring. As with many dimensions, this one is interconnected with others. Planning, procedures, content and student knowledge, expectations, and others are a part of this dimension.

In looking at the rubric, it is clear that a distinguished teacher does so well in other dimensions that behavior problems are rare and minor. This level teacher handles the behavior with no interruption of instruction, often by proximity or glance. The respect and support for everyone in the classroom is obvious, and it is evident in shared expectations.

An important component to reaching the distinguished level is using positive reinforcement. Recognizing behavior that is desired increases the likelihood that it will occur again. A distinguished teacher uses positive reinforcement to make clear the behavioral path that is needed for social and academic success. A respected teacher, at any grade level, who recognizes a student for work or behavior will quickly get most of the others to fall into line. It is a powerful tool.

Moving from proficient to distinguished in this dimension will require students' to respect the teacher. This is built through improvement within all T-TESS dimensions. Building positive relationships with students will help in creating shared expectations. These discipline expectations, along with the consequences of not meeting them, need to be communicated to both parents and the principal. Awareness within these groups will be important to the overall success of the plan.

# Classroom Culture

*The teacher leads a mutually respectful and collaborative class of actively engaged learners.*

There are principals who say that they can tell if a classroom is effective within 30 seconds of walking into it. The tone and environment provide immediate feedback to the visitor regarding the mutual support for learning that exists. A walk-through observation that finds a classroom with students engaged in collaborative work, a level of purposeful student discussion creating a level of ambient noise, and a teacher moving from group to group in order to prod greater depth, is one that creates positive feeling in the observer. It does not take long to recognize a strong classroom culture.

In contrast, classrooms that have students trying to get attention in ways not related to the work, or instructors sitting behind their desks, is one that signals problems. Attention seeking of students suggests a lack of focus and engagement on the work, and teachers who are not in close proximity to students are limiting the overall effectiveness of any assignment. There can be other signs of culture issues, but these become obvious very quickly.

In fact, there is some research that suggests that classroom evaluations may not require long visits. Carey (2014) reported on a study that found a short interval of observing teachers aligned closely with the extended formal evaluation. This seemed to connect with the classroom culture. Details regarding the reason for the culture may require more time, but there is a feel that we all get.

The T-TESS is detail oriented on the specific areas (dimensions) that increase student learning, and it focuses on evidence to support these, so gaps will become more evident as principals start walk-throughs and script formal observations. Teachers who do well in the other dimensions are likely to have a supportive classroom culture.

## A Brief Look at 3.3 in Action

Teresa Young's seventh-grade reading class was working in groups as her principal walked into the room. He walked through several times a week, so everyone was accustomed to his presence. He enjoyed visiting Ms. Young's class because of the culture she had developed. The students worked collaboratively and supportively, and the level of engagement was impressive.

This visit had student groups involved in work differentiated on academic need, while the content of the text was relevant to the students' interests. One set of students were reading quietly to a partner, several others respectfully collaborated and encouraged each other as they worked on a writing assignment, and Ms. Young sat around a group for guided reading. By giving students the opportunity to choose what to read, from a preselected set of texts at the appropriate reading level, Ms. Young demonstrated awareness of her students' interests, thus enhancing her rapport and ultimately the classroom culture.

There was good student focus and purposeful collaboration, but after 20 minutes a few students were beginning to show obvious signs of mental fatigue. She brought the class together and debriefed with them what they were doing and switched group assignments. Student endurance was something she had worked on earlier in the year, and it was paying off. Everyone moved into their new assignment effortlessly, using their skills in a new context.

# The Big Three

The classroom culture embeds most of the other dimensions. You cannot have a good culture without efficient procedures, supportive teacher and students, high engagement, and parent connections, among others. However, the big three characteristics of a great classroom culture are as follows:

1. Student engagement is an important characteristic of learning in general, but it sets a tone that permeates the classroom. Engagement includes using time well (bell to bell), providing work of interest and meaning to the students, and ensuring that there is a connection to life. Along with being the foundation for a great culture, there is a strong correlation between academic engagement and achievement.
2. Teacher care embedded into effective procedures is important. Care is important, but being too friendly is not always helpful. Teacher care is based on what is best for the students, and that is wrapped in high expectations.
3. Teachers model some important behavior that leads to student support. A distinguished classroom culture has students that respect, support, encourage, and trust each other and the teacher.

# Points to Remember

- The teacher sets the tone through modeling of care and supportive behavior in an environment of high expectations.
- Caring teacher behaviors include showing compassion for students who do not fit in.
- A good culture has efficient and effective procedures in place.
- High expectations for academic performance and socio-emotional behavior set an appropriate tone in the classroom.
- Students who play a strong role in their own learning leads toward a distinguished classroom.
- Students have the opportunity to collaborate and encourage each other.
- Student support of the teacher and each other is evident.
- Assignments are engaging, relevant, and meaningful.

# The Administrative Lens

The principal may get an early impression of the culture, but evidence will be important to document. Questions to ask include:

- Are teachers and students supportive of each other?
- Do students feel comfortable to take risks?
- Is the noise in the room purposeful?
- Are assignments engaging and meaningful?
- Does the teacher exhibit care?

# Moving from Proficient to Distinguished

Classroom culture is difficult to define. It is kind of like Supreme Court Justice Potter Stewart trying to describe obscenity in 1964. In his classic statement, he stated that it was hard to create a list of characteristics, but "he knows it when he sees it." A good classroom culture is similar. There are highly compliant students in quiet, organized classrooms that do not have a culture that would be considered distinguished. But it could. It depends on the work assigned, support provided, and procedures in place, among other factors. Support does not indicate care, but it is hard to have a good classroom culture if the students do not feel as if the teachers care.

When going from proficient to distinguished, teachers must put systems in place that allow students to collaborate and encourage each other; they work in a positive learning environment and have ownership of their learning. Students in proficient classrooms are engaged in meaningful learning. While in distinguished classrooms, the learning is not only meaningful but also related to their interests. A strong understanding of differentiation and collaborative learning will help teachers seeking to move to the left of the T-TESS rubric. Distinguished teachers are committed, not just to earn respect, but to ensure mutual support among students occurs as they engage in relevant learning.

Distinguished teachers in this dimension will have to be scoring very high in classroom procedures, student engagement, monitoring, planning, and having students value education to the point of creating autonomous learners. A distinguished classroom culture is the most difficult to attain because it requires everything else to be great, plus a dose of artistic flare.

Carey, B. (2014). *How we learn*. New York, NY: Random House.

# Professional Practices and Responsibilities

**Dimension 4.1:** Professional Demeanor and Ethics

**Dimension 4.2:** Goal Setting

**Dimension 4.3:** Professional Development

**Dimension 4.4:** School Community Involvement

# Professional Demeanor and Ethics

*The teacher meets district expectations for attendance, professional experience, decorum, procedural, ethical, legal, and statutory responsibilities.*

The Texas Educators Code of Ethics, found in chapter 247.2 of the Texas Administrative Code, is an effort to codify the concept of "do the right thing." There are three main standards and 29 substandards that help provide clarification. To simplify the first standard, *Professional Ethical Conduct, Practices and Performance*, a teacher needs to be honest, responsible, and transparent. This takes care of most issues within any professional behavior. A teacher does not have to be perfect, but an unwillingness to take responsibility for behavior, or trying to cover it up, becomes unethical.

The second standard, *Ethical Conduct Toward Professional Colleagues*, involves similar traits, but mentions the importance of protecting confidential information. Generally speaking, a teacher should not lie, gossip, illegally discriminate, or retaliate against a coworker. The final standard, *Ethical Conduct Toward Students*, provides the same guidelines, along with others related to student age and subordinate status. These should not have to be said, but an educator commits an unethical, immoral, and illegal act by providing alcohol or having sex with a student. But there is a problem here, as the reported acts of student–teacher sexual relationships is at an all-time high.

One of the reasons that this is becoming a bigger problem is due to the increased ease of private communications that occurs in the electronic age. The guidelines on *Ethical Conduct Toward Students* addresses inappropriate communication, and most of it is related to social media and cell phones. Using texting and email to communicate with students has its place, and the standards recognize this, but the purpose of the communication is important. Sending a group text to students to let them know practice has been cancelled is probably fine if your local policies allow it. Sending a private email to tell a student he or she looks nice is a problem.

Students do not need a teacher to be a friend; they have enough friends. They need someone who cares about them, but also someone they respect. The teacher is available for support, but also knows where to draw the line. In high school, students can be the one who wants to get closer to a teacher on a personal level, which requires skills of tact and firmness in drawing this line.

Dimension 4.1 requires more than simply following the letter of the law, but the teacher must model ethical and legal behavior while always serving as advocates for their students. That being said, a teacher needs to have a good understanding of local policies, as well as state and federal laws. Most teachers know about Special Education and Family Education Rights and Privacy laws, but there are some that will be learned along the way. Asking administration about the legalities of any new initiative should be done in the planning phase.

## A Brief Look at 4.1 in Action

Joe Smith arrived at school at 7 a.m. to finish preparing the laboratory assignment for his middle school science class. He wore a lab coat to help protect his suit. He got into a habit of wearing a suit because it became evident that students responded a little better to him when he dressed professionally, and he was given more preference when speaking with other stakeholders. He had a saying that often got a laugh: "When I wear a suit, I don't have to be as smart."

As Mr. Smith looked finished preparing for the laboratory lesson, he glanced over his calendar for the day. He was discussing how he uses cooperative grouping in the Professional Learning Community meeting, and he had agreed to discuss the science curriculum at a stakeholder meeting after school. He expected a local political group to be there that did not like some parts of the curriculum. He was not looking forward to that, but he was going to honestly and transparently address their concerns. His ultimate purpose, as with all other behaviors of a professional educator, was to do what was best for the students.

# The Big Three

There are occasional issues with unethical behavior among teachers, but this is rare. Ninety percent of teachers do what they should do and model professional behavior. Remember these big three professional issues:

1. If there is bad news to tell, be the one to tell it. There is nothing that hurts the credibility of a professional more than appearing to hide information. Remember: Honesty and transparency is important.
2. The way you dress is an advertisement to the outside world of your professionalism. Be sure to dress professionally.
3. Teachers are leaders. Volunteer to lead PLCs and other professional development. Work to make the campus a better place for kids and be a student advocate.

# Points to Remember

- Read the *Code of Ethics and Standard Practices for Texas Educators*. It can be summarized by stating that teachers should be honest, open, transparent, and legal, but there are other intricacies within the document that should be known, so a good read is in order.
- Do what is right for kids.
- Dress to send the message to children that they are important.
- Be early for work every day, and stay late. This does not mean that a teacher needs to give up personal time, but the work of professional teaching is important. And once again, this sends a message.
- Have fun. Professionals love what they do, and enjoy it. Take the time to know your students and colleagues well enough that you enjoy seeing them.
- Be careful with electronic communication. There are legitimate reasons to text or email students, but make sure the local policies are followed.
- Use school resources for school business. Using school copiers, printers, etc. for personal business is unethical.
- Never be indifferent to bullying, harassment, or other behaviors that may harm students or colleagues.

# The Administrative Lens

An administrator collecting evidence to rate this dimension should consider:

- Does the teacher take a leadership role among colleagues?
- What type of message does the teacher's attire send?
- Does the teacher meet the district's attendance requirements?
- Are the *Code of Ethics and Standard Practices for Texas Educators* followed?
- Does the teacher know and adhere to local, state, and federal regulations?
- Does the teacher follow the district's electronic communications policy?
- How does the teacher advocate for students?

# Moving from Proficient to Distinguished

The terms used for proficiency in the T-TESS rubric are the same as those for being distinguished, so the level of performance is a matter of degree. The distinction is made between teachers that meet and those that model the standards. All teachers are expected to be ethical. A distinguished teacher will not only be ethical, but will be a leader on campus. This leadership will take the form of assisting colleagues in their professional activities and advocating for students campus-wide. A distinguished teacher takes passion outside of the classroom and influences individuals throughout the school system.

A distinguished teacher in professional demeanor and ethics recognizes that every behavior exhibited is a message being sent to students, parents, colleagues, and other stakeholders. A teacher who monitors the hallway while staring at a cell phone advertises that the students are secondary to the text being sent. Dressing in an ordinary way sets the tone that those being taught are not worth the teacher's best. Messages are sent with everything we do. Distinguished professionals recognize this and use it to their advantage.

There is one more sign of teachers who do well on this dimension. They have fun. High achieving professionals enjoy the challenge of being life-changing, and their creativity and passion becomes evident. These individuals learn to be "all in" with everything they do, and this becomes the foundation for greatness.

# Goal Setting

*The teacher reflects on his/her practice.*

There is a common story among motivational speakers that analyzes two groups of college graduates: One group wrote goals, and the other did not. Many years later, researchers looked at the success of the students. Across the board, students who had set goals were more successful in both career and family.

The accuracy of this story has been questioned (nobody can find the original source), but the basic point makes sense. Persons who know where they want to go professionally and personally are more likely to get there. This reflects a parable from the *Alice in Wonderland* tale:

Alice: "Would you tell me, please, which way I ought to go from here?"
Cat: "That depends a good deal on where you want to get to."
Alice: "I don't much care where."
Cat: "Then it doesn't matter which way you go." (Carroll, 1865)

Dimension 4.2 is about answering that question: "Where are you going?" Teachers who know where they are going should be able to provide long- and short-term professional goals to address improvement in both teaching and education in general, and consistently monitor and adjust practices based on the progress toward those goals. Furthermore, goal-driven teachers are aware of the impact their professional development have on their students' progress toward their learning goals. Not only should teachers be able to verbalize where they are going, but they also should have a plan on how to get there. A document addressing this might look at different domains identified through previous observations and shared concerns of administrators (areas of refinement), and heavily rely on personal reflection. The goals should be aligned to the T-TESS dimensions as well as the Texas Teacher Standards. When taking a brief look at Dimension 4.2 in action, you will find what a document outlining the teacher's professional goals might look like.

# A Brief Look at 4.2 in Action

Joseph Flanagan reflected on his teaching needs, and he realized, based on walk-throughs and other data, that he needed to get students more actively engaged in their educational process. In order to begin the process of goal setting, he scribbled the following:

**Dimensions:** Activities; Content Knowledge and Expertise; Classroom Culture

**Goal:** I will increase meaningful experiences in my classroom so I maximize instructional time and students are consistently engaged in learning that is relevant to life outside the classroom by implementing collaborative learning.

**Steps to achieve goal:**
1.  Attend ESC professional development on the design of collaborative learning lessons.
2.  Develop efficient classroom procedures for student-driven learning that supports relevant learning.
3.  Meet with and observe Mrs. Smith to see her implementation of collaborative learning.
4.  Design lessons where students work collaboratively on products that are standards-based and related to the real-world.

**Evidence used to determine goal achievement:**
*  Increased student engagement in standards-based learning that is relevant to them as measured classroom observations.

- Increased student mastery of the standards as measured by unit assessments, student work and state assessments.

Mr. Flanagan knew that there would always be components of instruction that would not include collaborative learning, but he believed his classroom would become more meaningful with more of it. His principal agreed that this would be a great goal, and they had discussed ways in which the administration could support him.

# The Big Three

A teacher wanting to score well in goal setting should pay particular attention to the following:

1. Always connect goal setting to observation and student performance data. Subjective reflection can provide some areas needing improvement, so do not discount that completely, but psychological studies suggest most people do not self-evaluate well. Pay attention to data collecting, such as student scores, surveys, discipline referrals, walk-through evaluations, and others in connecting to reflective areas of self-improvement.
2. Principals should be aware of areas in which they feel a teacher should improve. Teachers need to make some of their goals a shared process with their principals.
3. Students need to take ownership of their own learning, and similarly, teachers need to own their professional development.

# Points to Remember

- Goal setting helps set the professional direction of the teachers and should be targeted on the areas that have the most impact on student learning.
- Even the best teachers can get better. Work on it.
- Create goals based on performance measures, reflection, and shared understandings with the principal.
- If it becomes clear that there are problems with the goal or action steps to accomplish it, modify. There are few things worse that persistence in the wrong direction.
- Goals should be SMART: Specific, Measurable, Agreed upon, Realistic, and Time based.

# The Administrative Lens

An administrator who is leading a goal setting meeting and providing a teacher feedback related to his or her goals should consider:

- How will the teacher be supported in accomplishing goals through professional development sessions, walk-throughs, conferences, or other means?
- Is the teacher taking the lead in his or her own professional development?
- How are the professional activities impacting student learning?
- Are improvements in goals being seen in the classroom?
- Is there consistent reflection and data collection on the goals to determine if modifications are needed?
- What evidence related to student learning will be used to measure the attainment of the goals?

# Moving from Proficient to Distinguished

All professionals should be consistently improving their craft. This process has gotten formal for teachers within the T-TESS. Teachers aiming to be at the distinguished level in this dimension must go beyond goal setting and meeting those goals. Distinguished teachers consistently monitor their progress to modify goals as needed. They monitor the impact their professional development is having on student learning. Distinguished teachers work with their supervisors and colleagues in search for feedback. Additionally, distinguished teachers stay abreast of the latest research and analyze the impact their actions have on their students. These teachers use research-based practices and their analysis of student learning to make changes in instruction. Minor improvements, compounded over time, result in teachers that have an incredible impact on the achievement of students.

Teachers should review their professional goals regularly to see if they are meeting goals without modification, or whether some component of the goal or action plan needs to be tweaked. The professional goals process should be teacher-centered. Engaging in self-reflection is a key component of this dimension.

There should be differentiation of goals among teachers, because every individual has different strengths and needs. The range of possible goals is innumerable given that each descriptor within the T-TESS dimensions and every Texas Teacher

Standard have the potential to be a goal. It is important to remember that when developing professional goals, teachers should give priority to the dimensions or standards that would have the biggest impact on their teaching.

Teachers should be reflective on their professional needs while working with their appraiser through the goal-setting process. The goals should be shared with the principal, but the teacher must take personal responsibility for addressing the areas of need and providing evidence to support improvement. Teachers must take ownership of their own professional growth while counting on their appraisers' support.

One other recommendation: Goal setting should not include every possible professional recommendation. It should be targeted on the top three to four goals that will make the biggest difference professionally.

Carroll, L. (1865) *Alice's adventures in Wonderland.* New York, NY: Gramercy Books.

# 4.3

# Professional Development

*The teacher enhances the professional community.*

---

The T-TESS dimensions consistently lead to student autonomy in regard to learning, and Dimension 4.3 measures the same thing among teachers. Teachers who are distinguished in this dimension are both strong in professional development and leadership. These individuals are collegial and supportive of fellow teachers, recognizing opportunities for campus improvement. High achievers extend their professional influence beyond their classroom.

Teachers should be the leaders of the campus. As professionals, they should have a strong role in the development of the vision, and as part of this, the trainings in which they participate. Teachers have a wealth of education and experience, and many times are as knowledgeable about important subjects that need to be a part of campus training as any outsider. Distinguished teachers in 4.3 help develop other teachers through both formal and informal trainings.

Distinguished teachers that provide professional development on campus is only part of the dimension. All teachers are expected to constantly improve, so recognizing personal areas of need is important. This modeling is important for setting a campus tone of improvement.

Finding areas of improvement can be done through reflection, but as always, data is an important source of information. There are areas that can be identified as a campus-wide need. For example, low scores among special education students may be an indication that an overall plan, which includes training, needs to be developed. This creates a shared understanding of expectations and strategies for improving scores in the area of special education.

There are a number of areas in which data may be used at the campus level to determine professional development needs for all. Discipline records, test scores, participation rates, performance of student sub–groups performance, and others may have data that suggests the need for a common understanding for the campus. Distinguished teachers are recognizing and assisting with these campus achievement gaps.

# A Brief Look at 4.3 in Action

Ron Jones looked at his peers as the professional development began. He was a little nervous because this was his first time to speak as a teacher leader. His topic was cooperative learning, as he was recognized by his principal as being excellent at this teaching strategy. He became a likely expert to discuss it when a survey on campus stated that most teachers did not feel comfortable with students working in groups.

Mr. Jones, passionate about the topic, began to take the lead on increasing the knowledge and skills needed to increase teachers' comfort zone with cooperative groups. He had met with several PLCs, and had even worked with a teacher who requested his assistance in her classroom, but having everyone on campus staring at him was unnerving.

He started, "Cooperative grouping is a planned and purposeful instructional strategy … ." He continued with an activity in which the teachers were divided into cooperative groups. His first experience as a teacher leader was going well.

# The Big Three

The big three areas to remember in professional development are:

1. Modeling professional improvement through personal goal setting, reflection, and data analysis is an important first step to influencing the campus.
2. All teachers have areas of expertise that can be used to improve the performance of a campus. Distinguished teachers are leaders who use their gifts to impact others.
3. Analysis of data is important in determining campus professional development needs. Gaps or low performance may be a signal that training opportunities need to be developed for the campus.

# Points to Remember

- Professional development is a contact sport. It occurs with colleagues and requires interaction.
- Teachers need to move out of the classroom and share expertise with others.
- Analysis of data is important in finding professional development needs on a campus.
- Professional development strategies will be outlined within the campus improvement plan.

# The Administrative Lens

An administrator collecting evidence to rate this dimension should consider:

- How involved is the teacher in PLCs and other collaborative meetings?
- Does the teacher assist in fulfilling the strategies of the campus improvement plan?
- Does the teacher help others in professional development?
- Are resources being used effectively and efficiently?
- Is reflection and data analysis used in determining professional development?

# Moving From Proficient to Distinguished

A teacher moving from proficient to distinguished in this dimension will have to move from the confines of the classroom to become a leader on the campus. This means more than just grade- or subject-level PLC leadership; it will include promoting the goals of the campus through the improvement of professional development.

These types of teacher leaders will work with the administration to analyze data, plan trainings, and generally support improvement plans. Teachers who have met this level will often lead campus-wide professional development, as getting to this point indicates a level of curriculum and instructional expertise that is exceptional.

# School Community Involvement

*The teacher demonstrates leadership with students, colleagues, and community members in the school, district, and community through effective communication and outreach.*

A teacher once told a story to a group of his peers, and it went like this: There was a dad who annually went to the school, and his purpose was to complain about the incompetence of the teachers. He was an angry man, and his fits left everyone perplexed and concerned. One day, he entered the school to meet with a teacher who had sent a congratulatory letter home. The letter discussed the progress of his child, and it thanked the father for his influence in the child's life.

The dad pulled out the letter before talking to the teacher. He said that much of it was difficult to understand (he did not read well), but he saw the word "congratulations." The teacher explained the letter, and the father thanked him and quietly walked out.

The dad continued to go to the school, but his behavior was much better. He was supportive of the teachers, and seemed to want to create a connection. There was a rumor that he had started a new medication, but the teacher who wrote the letter knew better.

Great teachers understand their role in creating a good professional relationship with students and the students' parents. These teachers begin communicating with stakeholders long before the relationship becomes important for a stressful situation, like with discipline. Most believe a good relationship makes a discipline discussion unlikely to be needed.

One of the strategies typically used by these great teachers is to send specific, sincere notes of praise home to parents. There is nothing more important to parents than their children. They all want to think the best of them and they will think highly of a teacher who recognized their child's talents.

These notes stay on the refrigerator for months and will be a constant reminder of the value you place on the student. This planning and preparation for communication in an important component of school community involvement, and it is an important part of the process of developing professional relationships.

Once this foundation is developed, pushing the student to pursue higher goals is more likely. An involved parent increases the likelihood of an academically engaged student.

## A Brief Look at 4.4 in Action

David Smith recognized the importance of involvement from all stakeholders within his sixth-grade band class. He recruited students who were reluctant to join band, regularly praised hard work, and consistently found ways to get parents involved. John Davidson, principal of the middle school, heard more about these efforts in the post-conference discussion, but he was already aware of many strategies used from day-to-day interactions with Mr. Smith.

Parent involvement, Mr. Smith explained, was initiated and supported by several means. First, at least three students a week received a handwritten note, mailed home, that discussed something good the parents' child was doing in class. These notes were sincere, specific, and succinct, so they took less that 10 minutes a week to complete. Mr. Smith felt these may be the most important 10 minutes he spends, in part because of the feedback he received from parents, but also due to the improved behavior among students.

Mr. Smith invited parents to attend class twice each semester so they could hear the improvements being made in the musical performance. These classes were a time that parents and students alike valued, and Mr. Smith made sure to follow up with a quick email to each parent individually to thank them for their support. Many teachers who heard about these emails simply said there was not enough time to do something like this, but Mr. Smith had a shortcut. He had parent emails in a database, and he sent each person the same sincere thank you note that just had to be written once. Although not personalized, a follow-up thank you email had increased ongoing parent participation by 60%.

Mr. Smith explained to the principal that his performances at the school board meetings were to connect with groups peripheral to the campus, and Mr. Davidson was appreciative of the comments the board shared with him regarding these performances.

Finally, Mr. Smith discussed the community performances that the sixth-grade band held each fall and spring. They were well attended, in part due to the foundation that had been set on an ongoing basis. The students, parents, administrators, board members, and community at-large were proud and supportive of the young students that performed, and the larger outcome was a large and successful high school band. This band competed successfully in numerous contests, and a large number of these students continued playing in college.

## The Big Three

Teachers often find it difficult to communicate with parents and community. There are both time and emotional factors involved. These concerns can be minimized with the following big three characteristics:

- Regularly take the time to build positive relationships with parents and other stakeholders. This can be done easily and efficiently. A sincere letter home to parents that gives positive recognition to their child will go a long way toward creating goodwill between the school and home.
- Remember that there is nothing more important to parents than their child. This means that some parent responses are not going to be rationale. However, if you have built a positive relationship ahead of time, sensitive issues will be easier to handle.
- No one likes to be ambushed with bad news, so if something unusual is going on with a student, make sure the parents are aware.

# Points to Remember

- Carrying out a plan to build relationships with parents and students is important. This should be done long before any tough discussions (discipline, academic standing, etc.) are had.
- Be open, but tactful, with parents in regard to the progress of their child in regard to academic and social progress.
- Do not be the best kept secret in your district. Take opportunities to have your students perform, interact, and display work for the community.
- Be organized and prepared for Meet the Teacher Night and Open House. This is an easy way to look good for parents. One other note: Parents are less likely to come to a high school parent night, so create incentives to get them there, and make them feel valued once there.

# The Administrative Lens

An administrator providing evaluation to a teacher and looking for content should consider:

- Does the teacher have a plan for involvement with parents and community?
- Is the teacher prepared when the school has a parent involvement activity?
- Do parents know the progress of their child?
- Do parents and community members respect the teacher?
- Is there evidence of positive notes home to parents on a regular basis?

# Moving From Proficient to Distinguished

Generally speaking, schools do a poor job of building school community relationships. Teachers often lament the passing of the good ole' days when students who got in trouble at school would get twice the lashings at home. Those were the days, the story goes, when parents would support teachers, no questions asked.

Instead of lamenting the passing of these times, teachers can create them again through a planned and systemic method of communication. The foundation of this plan is trust, which can be built by recognizing the good in the most important thing in a parents' life, their child. Parents are usually not blind to the challenges that can occur with their child, but a positive note sends a message of caring about his or her educational outcomes.

Sending the message of care means that any concerns about behavior, academics, social interactions, etc. will be met with more attention from the parents. Parents want to know what is going on with their child, even the bad stuff, but knowing that the teacher cares makes any concerns easier to take.

A distinguished teacher understands this and has a plan for regular contact using multiple methods. This may include mail, email, social media, and other means (in line with local policies). This teacher assertively encourages participation in both parents and community members to provide ongoing support for student achievement. Getting everyone committed to high expectations for academic and socio-emotional performance will increase the likelihood for success.

CPSIA information can be obtained
at www.ICGtesting.com
Printed in the USA
FSHW011849190620

9 781524 911881